MAKING WAVES

MAKING WAVES

A Woman in This Man's Navy

LOUANNE JOHNSON

St. Martin's Press
New York

Acknowledgments

Heartfelt thanks to Tom Dunne, Margaret Schwarzer, Ruth Nathan, Maryanne Mazzola, Hilda Kassel, Ernest Scott, Bob Spinrad, Dave Terry, Charlie Ohl, Andrea Aguirre, Evelyn Hodak, Ann Derrick, my husband, Mark Chow, and my parents, Bob and Shirley Johnson. For teaching me; for believing in, encouraging, and advising me; for editing, marketing, publishing, and reviewing my work.

MAKING WAVES. Copyright © 1986 by LouAnne Johnson. All rights reserved. Printed in the United States of America. No part of this book may be used or reproduced in any manner whatsoever without written permission except in the case of brief quotations embodied in critical articles or reviews. For information, address St. Martin's Press, 175 Fifth Avenue, New York, N.Y. 10010.

Design by Paolo Pepe

Library of Congress Cataloging in Publication Data

Johnson, LouAnne.
    Making waves.

        1. Johnson, LouAnne. 2. Seamen—United States—
Biography. 3. United States. Navy—Biography.
4. United States. Navy—Women. 5. United States.
Navy—Sea life. I. Title.
V63.J64A3 1986   359′.0088042 [B]   86-17708
ISBN 0-312-50813-1

First Edition

10 9 8 7 6 5 4 3 2 1

MAKING WAVES

1

Mama Made Me Do It!

The eagle on her left sleeve glared at us as Petty Officer Pikes crossed her arms over her flat chest and surveyed her latest busload of recruits.

"Shut yer traps, put out those smokes, spit out that gum," she said. "You're in the Navy now, ladies, and you will do everything—eat, sleep, walk, talk, inhale and exhale—on my order." She spoke softly, but with unmistakable authority. "I'm your company commander. You will address me as 'Ma'am.' "

PO Pikes rocked from one foot to the other as she talked, her shiny black oxfords squeaking in rhythm with her voice.

"If you want to be in *my* Navy, if you want to wear The Blue, you're going to have to earn that right." She paused to give each one of us a quick once-over. When her cool blue eyes swept over me, I had the uncanny feeling that she had accurately sized me up in that brief moment. She knew I was having second thoughts. The rhythmic squeaking resumed. "Most of you will graduate from basic training, but some of you won't because you are quitters," she said, looking straight at me. "You're going to have to work harder than you ever have in your life. And you're going to find out that you have talents, skills, and strength that you never dreamed you had."

She was right. Until I joined the Navy, I had absolutely no idea that my bladder was so strong. The three cups of coffee I had drunk on the airplane were calling to me, but I was certain that PO Pikes would not appreciate it if I interrupted her introductory speech to ask if I could go to the bathroom.

"Welcome to basic training, ladies. This is your home for the next ten weeks." PO Pikes made sweeping gestures with both arms, indicating our new "home," which consisted of two long rows of green corrugated plastic cubicles, each containing two sets of bunk beds.

"I suggest you pay attention," she said, "because we do things a little differently here. There is a right way, a wrong way, and the Navy way. I'll teach you the Navy way, and you'll find your life much, much easier if you cooperate with me. You can't call your mommies and daddies to rescue you." I glanced around the barracks. She was right again. There wasn't a telephone—or a radio, TV, newspaper, or magazine—in sight. "If you screw up, you'll be very, very sorry. Believe me."

I believed her. I couldn't call my mother for help, anyway. She was the one who got me into this predicament.

When Mom first suggested that I enlist, I screamed, "What? And take more orders? After living with My Father the Dictator for eighteen years, you think I should join the Navy? Are you crazy?"

My father ruled our household with an iron hand and a black leather strap which he used to persuade his five rambunctious children to mind their manners. I planned on living an interesting life, bereft of manners, just as soon as I saved enough money to go to college. Given my salary as a stock clerk, and the rate at which tuition costs were rising, I figured that by the time I was forty-five, I'd have enough money to pay for my freshman year.

"The Navy will pay for your college, honey, and they'll send you to specialty training to be a journalist," Mom said, as she dumped the sudsy water out of the dishpan and wiped the water droplets off the faucet. She knew I had made up my mind when I was in the sixth grade, after reading the story of Nellie Bly, to be a journalist when I grew up, but I didn't believe my mother's claim that the Navy taught journalism. Of course, Youngsville, Pennsylvania, is a long way from the ocean, so I had never seen any sailors except my uncle Bruce, who was a boatswain's mate during the war, but I had seen plenty of nautical movies on television. Sailors were always standing guard on huge boats that were tossed around the raging ocean, battling wind, rain, waves crashing over the railings, or returning enemy fire. Sailors in the movies were always men and they never went to college.

"Sure, they'll send me to college, Mom," I snickered. "I bet they'll buy me a sports car, too."

"I don't think they provide cars, dear," she said, ignoring my sarcasm. "But they will pay for your college. I saw a TV commercial that explains the whole thing and I sent for a brochure." She dried her hands on her apron and began to rummage through the grocery lists, Scotch tape, coupons, and green stamp books in the junk drawer next to the sink. "Here it is." She handed me a booklet illustrated with pictures of young Navy women towing airplanes, operating radar screens, and strolling past the Eiffel Tower. "It says here that you would even get to travel. Just think, you'd have a chance to see the world outside of Youngsville."

"Where do I sign?" I grabbed the brochure and flipped through the pages.

Youngsville is a nice though unexciting little town, the kind of place where everyone knows everyone else and no one locks their door. If your neighbors want to visit, they tap on the screen door, holler, "Hoo hoo," and walk right in. In more exciting places, people get their heads blown off for walking unannounced into someone else's home, because people in cities keep their doors triple locked and most of them don't know or care who their neighbors are. In Youngsville, the residents know everything there is to know about each other, including the entire history of each family, because the population consistently remains at a familiar fifteen hundred. Half of the kids in town grow up and marry their high-school sweethearts. They buy houses and have the obligatory two-and-a-fraction children. The other half pack their bags the day after high-school graduation and disappear until their twenty-year reunion, which they attend only if they get rich or famous in the meantime.

I loved my family too much simply to disappear, but I couldn't pass up the chance to meet new people, visit new places, and earn a tuition-paid college degree. So, I paid a visit to the local recruiting office. They didn't ship me out to see the world immediately. First, I had to prove that my brain and my bladder had sufficient military aptitude. After filling out a few hundred forms at the local office, I was sent to a big government testing center. They tested my grammar. They tested my mechanical aptitude. They tested my reading ability. They tested my urine.

While the lab checked my body fluids and the recruiter checked my answer sheets, I sat on a metal chair and checked out the gray surroundings. Everything was gray —the floor tiles, desks, filing cabinets, trash cans, tables, chairs. There were even pictures of gray ships on the walls. The only spot of color in the room was an American flag hanging over a picture of the President. Under his picture was a little plaque that read Commander in Chief. I guessed that interior decorating wasn't one of the specialty fields offered in the Navy.

4

Fashion design wasn't a military specialty either, from the looks of the people bustling about the office in their shiny black shoes. Men and women all wore exactly the same clothes: blue jackets, pants and ties, and stiff, white shirts. The men all had the same short haircuts, which really made them look alike. No wonder they had to wear name tags. Even their own mothers wouldn't have been able to pick them out of a police lineup.

My recruiter, Jean, dropped her pencil into her little gray pencil cup and smiled at me from behind her immaculate gray desk.

"Congratulations," she said. "You are fully qualified to enter any of the enlisted ratings. Here is a list of specialties that I would recommend for you." She handed me a sheet of paper that listed a variety of occupational specialties: yeoman, aviation storekeeper, electronics technician. "Do you think you would like administration, personnel, or intelligence?" she asked. "Or perhaps you'd like to enter a more nontraditional field such as aviation electronics." I glanced over the list.

"I don't see journalist on here," I said. "I want to be a Navy journalist."

Jean looked genuinely disappointed. "I'm sorry," she said. "Women are not allowed to enter that rating. It's for men only. Many of our ratings are restricted."

"You mean you have to be a man to be a journalist in the Navy?" I asked. "Pencils aren't too heavy for women to lift." Jean laughed and shugged her shoulders.

"We've been making some changes lately," she said, "but we haven't received permission to enlist women as journalists yet." Secretly, I was relieved. While I was waiting for Jean to grade my tests, I had been having second thoughts about joining an organization where everyone wore the same clothes. It would be kind of like working at

5

Burger King, except the uniforms weren't as snazzy.

"Well, thanks," I said, as I sidled towards the door. "A journalist is the only thing I want to be in the Navy."

Driving back home, I thought about my interview. I'd done well on the written tests and passed the physical exam. I even passed the mechanical aptitude test, thanks to my dad, the do-it-yourselfer. The tools pictured on the test were the same as the ones in his tool chest. I knew how to use most of them and I had no problem recognizing a Phillips screwdriver, a socket wrench, a ratchet, or a soldering iron. I could operate a table saw and a tractor, too. I even knew how to gap the spark plugs in my car. There was only one reason why I couldn't be a military journalist —I was a woman. Back in Youngsville, I told everybody that I wouldn't join the Navy even if they begged me to because it was full of tacky dressers with definite chauvinistic tendencies. Vocabulary skills being what they were, most of the local residents bit their lips and rolled their eyes, certain that I was referring to some sort of sexual perversion, which didn't surprise them at all. They'd heard tell of them city folk, all right.

About two weeks later, the phone rang as I was sitting in the kitchen, polishing off a quart of chocolate chip ice cream, trying to decide whether to watch "Dialing for Dollars" on TV or go outside and watch the grass grow.

"LouAnne, this is Jean, your Navy recruiter. I have permission to give you a guaranteed seat in journalism school after you complete basic training. Can you be ready to go in two weeks?"

I was just about to say no when I happened to glance at the bulletin board beside the phone. Mom had tacked up the Navy brochure and I was looking at a photo of a young woman driving a yellow truck that was towing an airplane. The caption read "Join the Navy. It's not just a job . . . it's an adventure." Then I pictured myself in my current job, placing new stacks of ladies' underwear on the shelves in the lingerie department of a local discount store. I decided that I could wear tacky clothes and cope with a little chauvinism if it meant they would teach me journalism and toss in a little travel, adventure, and a college education as added incentives.

"Aye, aye, ma'am," I said. I had watched Popeye cartoons for years, so I had a headstart on the Navy lingo. I looked forward to the opportunity to mingle with some real swabbies and nonchalantly insert a "Well, shiver me timbers!" into the conversation.

Sooner than you can swab a deck, I was Seaman Recruit Johnson, Company 58, standing in a large gray building in Orlando, Florida, at one o'clock in the morning, with fifty other young women, staring speechlessly at our new company commander, our "CC."

Suddenly, I was scared. When I signed the enlistment contract, I lived in my own, comfortable home, where I was a free person. Now, I was tired, hungry, and had to go to the bathroom, but I couldn't sleep, eat, or pee—I couldn't do anything—unless this woman said I could.

"You ladies look tired"—Petty Officer Pikes was winding down her welcome speech—"and I know you've all spent a long day traveling, so we'll save our bunk-making lesson for the morning. When I call your name, walk over there, quietly, in single file and sign the requisition list. Take two sheets, one pillow, one pillow case, and one blanket." She pointed to a bunk piled high with linen, blankets (guess what color!), and pillows. "You will be assigned your bunks in alphabetical order, four girls to a cube. Make your bunks, put on your pajamas, brush your teeth in the head down the hall—for those of you who didn't do your homework, there are no bathrooms in the Navy, we

7

have 'heads'—and hit your racks. Enjoy your beauty sleep, ladies, because you're going to need it."

We had been warned not to talk, so my cube mates and I quietly exchanged smiles like patients in the waiting room of a dentist's office as we got ready for bed. It was nearly two A.M. before I finished making my bunk and crawled between my crisp white sheets.

This isn't going to be so bad after all, I thought, in the two seconds I remained conscious after my head touched the pillow. They seem like reasonable people here, making sure we get clean sheets and a good night's rest.

About three minutes later, some idiot started blowing a bugle into a microphone.

"DA-DA-DA-DA-DA-DA!! OH-FOUR-HUNDRED. RE-VEILLE!! REVEILLE!! HIT THE DECK, LADIES!!!! THE PARTY'S OVER. HIT THE DECK!!!"

I didn't want to hit the deck. I wanted to hit the sadist who was blowing the bugle.

"HIT THE DECK, LADIES! This isn't summer camp. When you hear the call for reveille, you have thirty seconds to hit the deck, put on your slippers and robes, and toe the line in front of your bunks. When I say toe the line, I mean *toe the line.* All your pretty little toes will be lined up along the same crack in the tile. And you will stand at attention with your arms at your sides, your fingers together, palms facing inward, your heels touching, and your toes pointed at a forty-five-degree angle. You will keep your eyes straight ahead at all times. When you are at attention, you do not move. You may blink and you may breathe, *if* you insist."

From the tone of her voice, Petty Officer Pikes hadn't had enough rest, either. I pulled my weary bones out of the bed and quickly shuffled to stand in line, looking around at the other girls. When the veterans back home found out I was joining the Navy, they told me only whores and lesbians joined the service. I figured they were lying, because I was neither, and the other girls looked pretty normal, too. Everyone looked sleepy and slightly nervous, except the girl on my right.

Marva Jones was the tallest and blackest girl I had ever seen. Apparently, Marva was not impressed with her first taste of military life. She stood muttering under her breath, "Ain't no need for all this carryin' on. Jumpin' outta bed and standin' in a line at this crazy-ass hour of the mornin'. Probably woke me up to tell me some silly thing, too." Marva yawned loudly. "They always tellin' around here. Tellin' me to wake up when I ain't done sleepin'. Tellin' me when to go to the batroom. Ain't nobody gotta tell Marva Jones when to go to the batroom." She shook her head. "Mmm-mm. These people crazy for sure."

I stared at Marva, fascinated by her looks and her speech, when suddenly I realized that the room had grown very quiet. Petty Officer Pikes stood directly in front of me. When I turned my head to face forward, our noses touched. She didn't back up an inch.

"What is your name, recruit?" she barked. I could feel her breath on my face.

"LouAnne Johnson, ma'am," I squeaked.

"Well, Johnson," she spat, "do you think this recruit standing beside you is more interesting than I am?" Actually, I did. But I had a sneaking suspicion that it would be in my best interest to be tactful rather than honest when standing nose-to-nose with PO Pikes.

"No, ma'am."

"Do you think she can tell you what you need to know to graduate from basic training?"

"No, ma'am." I sure wished she could.

"Then I suggest you pay attention to me when I talk to

you," said the CC. "I also suggest that you quit eyeballing me when you're standing at attention. Keep your eyes looking straight ahead at all times. Is that clear, Johnson?"

"Yes, ma'am." She was the one who put her face in front of my eyeballs in the first place, but I restrained myself from pointing out that fact, mainly because I was scared senseless.

"You have cost your company precious time because I had to stop and have this lovely little chat with you. Now we will have to run to the chow hall and we'll have to eat very fast. And then we'll have to run to supply to get our uniforms. If anyone gets indigestion, it will be your fault, Johnson." I didn't think it was fair to make me responsible for the digestive well-being of a group of total strangers, but I decided to overlook it—just this once.

Petty Officer Pikes continued pacing up and down the aisle between the cubicles, pausing every few seconds to give a particularly nasty stare to a girl who dared to cough or fidget.

"Ladies," she said, "let this be a lesson to all of you. You are no longer individual people. You are part of this company. If one person is late, you are all late. If one person breaks a regulation, you are all guilty. You will find that your lives will be much easier if you help one another." She paused, then clapped her hands.

"Now, hit those showers on the double. Get dressed, make your bunks, and hit the line. You have ten minutes. MOVE! MOVE! MOVE!"

Group hygiene is a sure-fire icebreaker. There were only six showers, so we had to stand in line with just our towels to cover ourselves, as we waited our turns. Fear and haste erased any traces of modesty we felt about standing around naked with a group of strangers. Within minutes, we were talking and laughing as though we were the best of friends.

Thirty minutes later, we were finally ready to go. No one wanted to be the last person to toe the line and be responsible for holding up the whole company, so the last few girls kind of hung around and jumped into line at the same time. We had some quick learners in our group.

"MUSTER!!!" PO Pikes yelled.

No one moved. "Muster" was an unfamiliar word, so we all stood at attention as the CC explained, in much more detail than I really cared to hear, an interesting new concept. When she called "Muster!" we had to drop what we were doing, rush outside to the sidewalk, and get in line from shortest to tallest in three even lines. Each person had to be directly in line with the persons in front of and beside her. The lines had to be *perfectly* straight and *exactly* one arm's length apart, both frontwards and sideways. Of course, the women in the line had arms of different lengths, so we had to set the distance according to the arms of the people in the first row on the right. That's probably why one of the requirements for enlisting in the service is possessing two arms.

I figured we had to muster so that when the communists were sneaking around, trying to count the American forces, they wouldn't be able to tell whether there were one hundred people or one person in the line, because the line would be so straight they could only see the person on the end.

We mustered and ran to the chow hall, where hundreds of male and female recruits were already standing in line at parade rest, with their hands locked behind their backs and their feet spread slightly. I don't know why we had to run—we had to stand there for twenty minutes, smelling the pancakes and bacon, watching other people file in and out. It didn't make sense to me, but I soon realized that making sense isn't one of the objects of recruit training.

Our turn finally came and we marched single file into the chow hall and picked up gray trays piled high with plates of steaming eggs, bacon, pancakes, and sausages. Hungry as we were, we couldn't sit right down and dig in. Oh, no. Recruits have to eat as companies, so we lined up along the gray benches at the gray tables and sniffed our food as we waited permission to eat. If they had made us share silverware so we could really experience togetherness, I was going to tell PO Pikes that I thought they were carrying things a little too far. Lucky for her, we each got a fork.

Several companies of male recruits filed by us as we stood waiting. They stared at us like they'd never seen females before. They looked at everything but our faces and made loud comments about our anatomies—comparing us to their food, saying how juicy and delicious we looked. Talking to males, even looking at them, was strictly forbidden to female recruits. Any girl caught talking to a man during basic training got a handful of demerits and a chance to scrub the barracks floor with a toothbrush.

"Sit!" screamed our CC. Four minutes later, she screamed, "Ah-ten-HUT!" and we had to stop eating. Our delicious food went back to the kitchen, barely touched, and we rushed outside, still hungry.

"There's no time for leisurely brunches here, ladies," Petty Officer Pikes explained as we lined up outside the chow hall. "When the last person in your company sits down, you have five minutes to eat your meal. You will be surprised how much you can eat if you concentrate. Don't worry, lunch is only six hours away."

I knew why we had to eat so fast. Digestion is simply not as important as our national defense. Our military people have to be prepared to defend our country on a moment's notice, always remaining alert and watchful. We can't have the troops sitting around dunking doughnuts into their milk mugs when the commies attack. Hungry people are probably meaner, too.

No one got indigestion from the running, but there was a lot of burping going on as we mustered after Lesson No. 1 in Speed Eating.

Enroute from the chow hall to the supply department, PO Pikes taught us our first marching song:

We're women in the Navy,
We march with pride.
We march shoulder to shoulder
And side by side
On our left, our leh-eh-eft, on our left.

The feet in our company had quite a problem matching the songs. One girl was almost six feet tall and the shortest was under five feet. Try as they might, they just couldn't seem to march to the same beat. PO Pikes thoughtfully offered subtle little hints about which feet we should be stepping on while marching. She ran along beside us, screaming, "Left, right and left," which sounded more like "Lef, rye oh lef." No one paid attention to her, but that didn't daunt her enthusiasm.

The supply department looked like a huge clothing store, except that all the clothes were baggy and blue. We got little blue wool hats that looked like the kind soda jerks used to wear. We got ugly blue baggy pants, white shirts, black ties, and navy-blue sweaters. And we got the ugliest black leather oxford shoes that ever walked on this planet. My grandmother would have enlisted just for those shoes! We're talking disgustingly sensible.

Our real Navy uniforms were stuffed into huge duffle bags which we had to lug back to the barracks so there would be plenty of clothes to wash, fold into squares, iron, and inspect for the next nine weeks. If we weren't bored to death before then, PO Pikes promised we'd get to wear the real uniforms, just like the big kids, for the last week of training.

Each recruit was also issued a ditty bag containing black shoe polish, cotton balls, and big black marking pens. As soon as we returned to the barracks—marching and singing, of course—we were instructed to write our last names on every single item we had in our lockers. Last names only. They took away our first names along with our civilian clothes.

Writing my name on my towels reminded me of summer camp. In fact, basic training is a lot like summer camp. Some crazed idiot blows a bugle to wake you up at an ungodly hour in the early morning, you play games, wear ugly clothing made of sturdy materials, tromp around singing songs, sleep in bunk beds, and write your name on all your underwear. The difference is that the campers at basic training sign contracts, agreeing to let people scream at them in exchange for a weekly paycheck.

At first, I took it personally when PO Pikes screamed in my face. Then I remembered what my uncle Bruce, who had been in the Navy, told me. He said that I should remember that my job was to get yelled at and do what I was told, especially if it didn't make any sense. He also said I should remember that my company commander's job was to yell at us. She only had ten weeks to turn a bunch of normal, sloppy civilian women into neat, orderly sailorettes who ate real fast and marched around with unnaturally good posture.

Once our underwear was properly named, we received

our locker instructions. All our clothes had to be folded exactly the same way, with the folds going in the same direction. Everything had a specific place to sit on a particular shelf. I had to laugh when I read the instructions— there was a whole page explaining how we were to fold our underwear into neat little squares. I had just left a job in the lingerie department in search of adventure and here I was folding underwear again.

It took us hours to "stow" our lockers according to our written instruction pamphlets. Except for Marva Jones. Within minutes, she finished stowing her locker, which was next to mine, and spent the rest of the time walking around watching other people work, telling jokes and enjoying herself.

After Lesson No. 2 in Speed Eating, it was time for our first locker inspection. Petty Officer Pikes came around with a clipboard and checked to see if we had followed her instructions to the letter. Of course, none of us had good scores. But the CC gasped when she opened Marva's locker. Clothes were tossed every which way, some on the shelves, others hanging from hooks. Underwear was rolled into balls and stuffed into Marva's shoes.

"Jones!"

"Yes'm." Marva stood looking down at Petty Officer Pikes, who was about a foot shorter than the recruit.

"Do you call this locker 'stowed'?"

"Yes'm."

"I know you can read, Jones, or you wouldn't be a recruit. But can you follow simple instructions?"

"Yes'm."

"Then why isn't your locker stowed properly?"

"Ain't nobody gotta tell Marva Jones how to fold her underwear. I knows how to keep my things. Ain't no need to be folding panties into little squares." Marva remained calm, stifling a yawn as she answered. The CC's eyes bulged out of their sockets and I could see her pulse pounding in the veins of her neck.

"Jones, you report to my office immediately following evening chow. Do you understand?"

"Yes'm."

After inspection, we all went into the lounge for a company meeting. Petty Officer Pikes told us to be "at ease." For the first time in two days, we were allowed to talk to one another and look around without being screamed at. It was our first chance to really get acquainted. Each of us had to stand up, say our name, tell where we were from and why we joined the Navy.

Some of the girls were like me; they wanted to travel and go to college. Others joined because their fathers had been career sailors and they wanted to carry on a family tradition. A couple of the older girls were recently divorced but had never worked, so they enlisted to learn job skills.

"I joined the Navy because my papa kicked me out of the house the day I turned seventeen," said one skinny, big-eyed girl. "He said he has too many mouths to feed and I'm old enough to get a job and take care of myself. But I don't aim to be a waitress all my life—I want to make something of myself. So I joined the Navy and I'm gonna learn a trade and have me a career."

"Ah joined the Navy 'cuz mah recruiter tol' me that I could get me a good job with the trainin' I'll get here. But he *didn't* tell me I was gonna have to go through all this craziness 'fore I got a job. I thought I was comin' here to work and here I am foldin' my panties and standin' in line in my pajamas." Everybody laughed at Marva's little speech except the CC. She cleared her throat and waited until we stopped giggling, then asked for volunteers to be Training Petty Officers. They wouldn't be real petty offi-

16

cers, but they'd be in charge of helping PO Pikes lead the company in various aspects of training. We had a Mail Call Petty Officer to pick up our life-sustaining letters from home, an Athletic Petty Officer to encourage us to keep doing sit-ups instead of napping on the gymnasium floor, a Mustering Petty Officer to scream "Muster" so we could run outside and line up on the sidewalk, and a Singing Petty officer to lead the little ditties we sang as we marched.

Finally, we were allowed to go to sleep. As I lay in my bed, listening to the bugle blowing taps, it dawned on me that the next nine and one-half weeks might very well be the longest I had ever lived. I had never realized how many minutes were in a day until I spent so many of them folding my underpants into perfect little squares, marching everywhere I went, and standing at attention listening to my stomach growl.

As usual, the CC had given us ten minutes to take showers, brush our teeth, and clean the entire head until it shone. As I brushed my teeth, I recalled the dental hygiene class we'd attended earlier that day. A petty officer had brought out a two-foot-tall plastic tooth and showed us how to brush and floss our teeth to prevent plaque. I appointed myself the Flossing Petty Officer and stood just inside the bathroom door with my roll of dental floss.

"Brush and floss, ladies, brush and floss," I chanted. "Cavities and bad breath are not authorized by Uncle Sam. If you want to be in my Navy, you'd better floss your teeth. Plaque is like communism—you have to fight it every day or it will sneak up on you and rot your teeth. So brush and floss, everyone. This message was brought to you by your local Flossing Petty Officer on behalf of the U.S. Navy." Then I stood at attention and hummed a few bars of "Anchors Aweigh" for added inspiration.

17

As I turned to leave the head, I bumped smack into the CC. She looked me in the eye, raised one eyebrow, and said, "Hope you didn't forget to floss, Johnson."

"No, ma'am. I flossed." She kept staring at me. *Please, God, make her hard of hearing.*

"Good." She walked on towards her office.

Thank you, God. I owe you one.

"Oh, Johnson!" To my dismay, PO Pikes was walking back towards me.

"You seem to have a lot of energy tonight, so I have a suggestion," she said. "Why don't you go back in there and clean all the toilets again just to make sure that they're spotless? Dirt is like communism, you know, Johnson. You have to fight it every day or it will sneak up on you. Don't you agree?"

"Yes, ma'am."

Apparently, even God wasn't authorized to help recruits.

2

Don't Talk
to the Trees

The barracks was pitch black by the time I finished scrubbing the toilets. I crept to my cubicle, undressed, and hung my clothes on the bedpost, which would cost me five demerits if the CC saw them in the morning, but my locker door was warped and it always clanged like a hammer hitting a piece of sheet metal when I opened it. I didn't dare break the silence in the barracks, where the only sound was the breathing of Company 58. Talking was absolutely forbidden after lights out, although we were usually too exhausted to make conversation, anyway. Everyone was either asleep or lying quietly in her bunk. Except Marva Jones. She stayed in bed just until the CC came around to make sure that we were all tucked safely into our cozy little gray bunks.

"Hey, Johnson, are you sleepin'?" Marva stood beside my bed, peering down at me.

"Shh!" I whispered. "You're supposed to be in your rack. You're gonna get in trouble."

Marva pooh-poohed me with a wave of her long, slender hand.

"Oh, don' you worry 'bout that," she said. "The CC done gone off to her own bed. I swear that woman got to be tired after chasin' us aroun' all day long, screamin' and hollerin' and carryin' on like she does."

"I'm tired, Marva," I said, yawning in hopes that my yawn would be contagious. "Why don't you go to sleep?"

"Ain't nobody gonna tell Marva Jones when to go to sleep." Marva wasn't about to yawn. "I goes to sleep when I'm tired and I jus' ain't tired right now. I'll jus' go talk to some of my new friends, Johnson. Don't pay me no min'. You go to sleep."

She walked from cube to cube, telling jokes and making everyone giggle. It wasn't long before a stern-faced petty officer stalked into the room. People were on guard all over the place, to keep us from climbing over the fences and going home during the middle of the night. My cube mates and I had discussed that very idea, but we concluded that since we had signed contracts promising to stay in the Navy for four years, they'd probably track us down and bring us back as permanent recruits, so we decided to do our best to stick it out.

The petty officer marched over to Marva. "Recruit!" she whispered sternly. "Hit the rack! You are not permitted to leave your rack after lights out unless you have to go to the head! Get in that rack!"

Marva didn't even break stride. She continued walking around. "Ain't nobody gotta tell Marva Jones when to go to bed. I knows when I's tired. I jus' ain't tired right now." She waved both hands at the petty officer, as though shooing a pesky child. "Go on, now. Maybe in a little while I'll be sleepy, but right now I'm jus' talkin' to a few of my friends. We never get a chance to talk durin' the days, you know." The petty officer blinked several times, unable to believe that she had just been dismissed by a recruit.

"Hit that rack!" she said through gritted teeth, no longer whispering. "You have ten seconds to get into bed or you're going to be very sorry. You already have fifteen personal demerits right now." She brandished her official clipboard. "And your company gets five demerits for your behavior. Would you like to try for more?"

"Okay. Okay." Marva sighed with disgust. "You don't have to get nasty an' take it out on the ladies here. I guess I could go to sleep jus' this once when I ain't tired. Good night, ladies!"

The next morning, Marva was gone. I saw her only once more, a few weeks later, marching with a brand new company of recruits, singing and laughing. She didn't seem to mind having to start over, even though that meant she would spend at least another week at boot camp. I never could tell if she was just dumb or if she was dumb like a fox. She told me that she had never had her own bed before —she always had to share with two or three sisters. And it was a real luxury for her to get three meals a day. I guess she didn't care if she kept getting sent back to start over. The longer she stayed in basic training, the longer she got fed and taken care of, without any responsibility on her part.

Marva wasn't the only one in our company who found basic training a vast improvement over her former life. One night at dinner, I sat next to a skinny girl from Tennessee named Maybell. No one at the table could understand a word she said because of her accent. We were all starving, since we usually had only four or five minutes to eat our meals, but amazement outweighed hunger and everyone at the table stopped eating and stared when Maybell attacked her food. She ignored her silverware and picked up a piece of meat with one hand. She tore a large hunk off with her teeth, and grabbed a healthy handful of mashed potatoes with her other hand. She stuffed the potatoes into her mouth and washed them down with a swig of milk. When the CC called a halt to chow time, most of us had eaten only a few bites from our plates, but

Maybell's was literally licked clean. She sat back, burped, and smiled at the girls around her.

Maybell had grown up in an environment where children weren't bothered with unnecessary things like knives and forks. Unfortunately, they weren't troubled by having to learn to read, either. Someone must have helped Maybell fill out the enlistment forms, but she wasn't able to read any of our class assignments, so they sent her back to Tennessee. It took about two weeks for the discharge papers to be processed, so at least she got to eat her money's worth before she left.

Lucky for me, I grew up in the cosmopolitan town of Youngsville, Pennsylvania, where everyone uses silverware and most people read. But there was one major deficiency in my education—I never did learn to handle a steam iron. I come from a long line of permanent-press women. My mom hated to iron, too, so when we were in high school she used to put all our clothes that had to be ironed into separate ironing bags for me and my two sisters. After three years, my bag of wrinkled clothes was still untouched, so Mom gave the clothes to the Salvation Army and I joined the synthetic-fabric fashion circle.

My carefree lifestyle came to an abrupt end when I found that we had to iron all the cotton uniforms that had been rolled up and crammed into our duffle bags. Since I didn't have three years to wait for the CC to pass my shirts on to some needy recruit, I resigned myself to the fact that I would have to learn to iron. Painstakingly, I ironed the front of one shirt, but when I turned it over, I found that I'd ironed a mass of wrinkles into the back. I ironed the back and turned it over again, only to find the wrinkles had somehow sneaked around to the front.

I glanced around the laundry room, but no one else seemed to be having any problems. The girl on my left was humming softly as she deftly finished pressing her fourth shirt. I watched in fascination as her iron swiftly skimmed the surface of the shirt, miraculously removing each wrinkle. A peculiar burning smell forced me to turn my attention to the shirt collar which was smoking under my iron. As I frantically tried to rub off the burn mark, the five crumpled shirts at the end of my ironing board fell onto the floor.

Frustrated, I burst into tears and threw the burned shirt on the floor with my other shirts. "I can't iron!" I wailed. "I never could! No one told me I had to iron in the Navy. I thought we had to swab decks and paint bulkheads!"

I stomped back to my cubicle and pulled out my shoe polish and cotton. Maybe I couldn't iron, but I knew how to spit-shine a pair of shoes. Ever since I fell down and broke the edge off one of my front teeth when I was ten years old, I'd had a natural talent for anything that involved spitting. I was admiring the reflection of my teeth in the toes of my shoes when my cube mate, Doris Lucas, walked in and hung six impeccably ironed shirts inside my open locker.

"There you go, Johnson," she said. "I ironed your shirts. Piece a cake."

I was really surprised. Lucas was a compact brunette from Connecticut who hadn't said more than a few words to anyone since the start of training. Nothing seemed to faze her. She looked almost bored when we "toed the line" next to each other during inspections, apparently not even the teeniest bit afraid of the CC.

"Wow!" I ran to my locker to admire the shirts. They were perfectly pressed and I was impressed. "You saved my life! How can I ever thank you?"

Lucas immediately looked down at her feet. "Now that you mention it, you can shine these ugly shoes," she said.

"They stink." At our first inspection, Lucas hadn't laced both shoes exactly the same way. One was laced with the ties left over right, the other was right over left. The CC made her relace every pair of shoes in our company. After lacing two hundred shoes, Lucas was a real champion lacer, but she hated those shoes with a passion. She pulled off her oxfords, without untying them, and tossed them on the floor.

"It's a deal." We shook hands and grinned at each other, both of us happy to have found a friend. If there's anyplace in the world where you really need a friend, it's at basic training.

Lucas had an older brother in the Navy who gave her all kinds of tips and strategies for surviving boot camp. One of the tricks he taught her was how to make the towel at the end of her rack hang exactly straight. During inspections, the towel had to be folded exactly in half and hung over the metal bedpost with the ends exactly even. A regular towel just wouldn't hang perfectly straight because it was too light. If someone walked past it, it would move just a little tiny bit in the breeze.

Lucas took my towel, folded it carefully in half and hung it over the end of my rack. Using clothes pins to hold it in place, she sprayed it liberally with a can of starch. After the starch had dried, she removed the clothes pins.

"There you go, Johnson. A petrified towel!" Lucas stood beaming with pride. "That towel won't move, I guarantee it. Just hope the CC doesn't bump into it—she might break her arm."

Lucas also taught me how to hide "geedunk" (candy, gum, etc.) in the barracks. We weren't allowed to have any snacks at all during basic training, except during the few minutes that the CC took us shopping at the exchange. As soon as we arrived in the store, we'd buy a bunch of junk

24

and cram it into our mouths as we strolled down the aisles, shopping for shoe polish, toothpaste, and other essentials. One day, Lucas bought a bunch of candy and brought it back to the barracks. After taps, we took the pillow off the bunk where Marva Jones used to sleep.

I stood guard at the door of our cubicle as Lucas removed the pillow case and tore a small hole in the end of the pillow. She put the candy into a plastic bag and stuffed the bag into the pillow, making sure that it was well cushioned and couldn't be felt by pressing on the pillow. She replaced the pillow case and returned the pillow to the bed.

"Aren't you afraid we'll get caught, Lucas?" I was nervous. I didn't want to get kicked out of the Navy for eating candy. What kind of story would that be to tell my grandchildren?

"You're such a wimp, Johnson," Lucas sighed. "If they find it, we just tell them it must have belonged to Marva. They'll believe us."

"You're so smart, Lucas."

"I know, Johnson. I know."

Fifty girls had started basic training in our company, but one by one the number dwindled to thirty. One girl was kicked out for cheating on exams, another one got caught trying to sneak into the men's barracks at night. Five girls flunked so many academic classes and physical fitness tests that the CC gave them back their civilian clothes and sent them packing. But the most interesting dropout was chubby Louella Jackson. Jackson went to the dispensary every day for one reason or another, but no matter what medicine she took, she was always sick. Whenever we marched, she lagged behind, complaining that her ankles were swelling up. She did well on her tests, so PO Pikes let her stay with us for about four weeks. Then the CC got fed up with all the medical visits and accompanied Jackson to the dispensary, refusing to leave until they found out what was wrong. Finally, the doctors reached a diagnosis. Jackson was seven months pregnant! When she came back to pack her bags and say goodbye to her shipmates, she told us that she didn't know how she got pregnant, that she didn't even know where babies came from. She sounded sincere, but they still wouldn't let her stay in the Navy. There isn't any designated space in the locker to keep a baby and, even if there was, a baby would undoubtedly scream real loud if someone tried to fold it up and square it away.

Jackson didn't know where babies came from, but most of the girls in our company were a little more worldly. One night as we were cleaning the barracks, Cindi Harmon nonchalantly mentioned that she used to work as a stripper. Of course, no one believed her. It was hard to imagine that this girl wearing baggy blue trousers, a shapeless shirt, and black oxfords could look like a sexy dancer.

"Sure, Harmon," one of the girls jeered. "All strippers are so patriotic that they join the Navy. Give me a break."

"I'll show you," Harmon said, as she jumped onto the top of a table.

She started doing a bump and grind dance, removing her uniform as she sang:

Beautiful Creamer, come unto me.
Make sure you hit me, so I will be
Pregnant as ever, then you will see
A cute little baby for you and for me.

The girls cheered and yelled, "Encore! Encore!" so she sang another song. This one really caught on and became our unofficial company song when the CC was out of hearing range.

He gave me inches one, inches one.
He gave me inches one, inches one.
He gave me inches one,
I said, "Darling, this is fun.
Put your belly next to mine and drive it on."

He gave me inches two, inches two.
He gave me inches two, inches two.
He gave me inches two,
I said, "Darling, I'm for you.
Put your belly next to mine and drive it on."

He gave me inches three, inches three.
He gave me inches three, inches three.
He gave me inches three,
I said, "Baby, you're for me.
Put your belly next to mine and drive it on."

He gave me inches four, inches four.
He gave me inches four, inches four.
He gave me inches four,
I said, "Honey, give me more.
Put your belly next to mine and drive it on."

He gave me inches five, inches five.
He gave me inches five, inches five.
He gave me inches five,
I said, "Man, are you alive!
Put your belly next to mine and drive it on."

He gave me inches six, inches six.
He gave me inches six, inches six.
He gave me inches six,
I said, "Babe, we're in a fix.
Put your belly next to mine and drive it on."

He gave me inches seven, inches seven.
He gave me inches seven, inches seven.
He gave me inches seven,

I said, "Darling, we're in heaven.
Put your belly next to mine and drive it on."

He gave me inches eight, inches eight.
He gave me inches eight, inches eight.
He gave me inches eight,
I said, "Baby, this is great!
Put your belly next to mine and drive it on."

He gave me inches nine, inches nine.
He gave me inches nine, inches nine.
He gave me inches nine,
I said, "Baby, you're divine.
Put your belly next to mine and drive it on."

He gave me inches ten, inches ten.
He gave me inches ten, inches ten.
He gave me inches ten,
I said . . . [*Pause*]
"Put your prick in your pants and drive me home!"

Ordinarily, such a vulgar song would have embarrassed me, but I wasn't feeling very friendly toward the male species on the night I first heard the catchy tune. Everywhere we had gone that day, the men screamed and whistled and hollered at us. But, if we even *looked* at them in response, we got demerits. It wasn't ladylike to respond to vulgar overtures, we were told. Men didn't exist as far as female recruits were concerned. In fact, they were referred to as "trees" by our CC.

"We don't talk to trees," she would remind us.

The men in one company managed to find out the name of a particularly pretty girl in our company who didn't happen to be particularly intelligent.

"Hey, Morgan!" a male recruit had yelled as we marched by that afternoon. Morgan automatically turned her head to look at him. Within seconds, a petty officer handed Morgan a report chit and she had to spend her rest hour that evening standing at attention in the middle of the sidewalk in front of the barracks, wearing a sign that said "I'm Stupid. I Talk to Trees." After that humiliation, she got five demerits. Twenty demerits meant a girl got recycled to a new recruit company, just like Marva Jones did. Morgan was a popular girl, so our whole company was mad at men in general.

That evening, the same company of men entered the chow hall just ahead of us. We had to stand beside their tables as we waited for our turn to be served. They undressed us with their eyes, which was bad enough, but they also made comments about every nasty thought that entered their dirty little minds.

"Look at the tits on that one!"

"Mmm. Mmm. How'd you like to eat that candy, boys?"

"That's why I joined the Navy—to ride those Waves!"

I could see the red face of the girl in front of me and I knew my own face was blushing just as hard, but we were forbidden to respond to the taunts. It wouldn't be ladylike. By the time we sat down to eat, I was completely humiliated, but inspiration struck. I whispered to the girl next to me to stare at the men's crotches as they filed past on their way out of the door. She passed the word down the line and soon we all sat, staring wide-eyed and innocent, at their crotches. It was hilarious. At first, the boys grinned, but when we didn't say a word or move our eyes from their private equipment, they started fidgeting and blushing, checking their zippers to see if they were down. We kept staring. They began dancing around, trying to stand so their backs were toward us. Their CC finally gave them the order to move out and started yelling that this one or that one was going to get demerits for fidgeting in line because he had been watching them.

29

They protested loudly, as our company was called to attention and mustered to leave. As we started to march off, I heard their CC yelling at our CC, "Hey, hold it! My men say your ladies were hassling them in the chow hall!"

PO Pikes couldn't hear what he said. I motioned her to continue marching forward. "It's okay." I said. "Go on. He's yelling at someone else."

Back at the barracks, we had a good laugh at the memory of the men checking their zippers and cupping their hands to hide their crotches, when Lucas pointed out that the male CC would undoubtedly call PO Pikes to see why she didn't stop when he yelled to her. Since it had been my idea to stare at the boys, the company unanimously voted that I should go have a little chat with the CC.

Shaking in my oxfords, I knocked on her door.

"Speak!" she barked.

"Seaman Recruit Johnson requests permission to speak to the company commander," I squeaked.

"Enter!"

I marched into her office and saluted in front of her desk. PO Pikes folded her hands on top of her desk and looked up at me. "Stand at ease, Johnson," she said. "What's on your mind?" She seemed to be in a good mood. She didn't frown, which was as good as a smile from a CC to a recruit.

I told her that I was curious. While we were in the chow hall, I had seen a company of men really harassing a company of women. Then I told her what the women did, omitting the minor fact that it was our company of women. Then I asked her if she thought those girls would get in trouble. PO Pikes didn't take her eyes off mine during my entire speech and I got the familiar feeling that she was reading my thoughts.

"Well, Johnson," she said, after several excruciating silent seconds. "Certainly you know that Waves are expected to conduct themselves in a ladylike manner at all times, so that kind of behavior is unacceptable." A hint of a smile tickled the corners of her mouth as she added, "However, under the circumstances, I don't think the ladies would get in too much trouble."

"Thank you, ma'am." I was so proud of myself for managing to explain the situation without letting her know it was her company that was involved that I stood smiling dumbly at her until she cleared her throat.

"Is there anything else, Johnson?"

"No, ma'am." I was suddenly anxious to get out of her office.

"Carry on." She nodded curtly, back to business.

I saluted, executed a snappy about-face, and marched out. Just as I reached the doorway, the CC spoke.

"Johnson!"

Another about-face. "Yes, ma'am?"

"Don't try it again," she said, her smile no longer in sight. "I wouldn't think it was amusing a second time."

"Yes, ma'am!"

We were pretty lucky that the CC decided to overlook our behavior. She was constantly reminding us to be ladylike, because any one of us might be the only Navy woman a civilian would ever meet. If we didn't act nicely, they would automatically assume that all Navy women were uncouth.

Just in case we had forgotten to bring our couth with us, we had classes in Etiquette. We weren't trained in standard international etiquette where you learn to eat salad with the little fork and keep your napkin in your lap and your elbows off the table. Instead, they taught us how to walk without swinging our hips and other interesting social skills. Our Etiquette instructor, Miss Beasley, was a tall, skinny, shapeless lady who spoke through her nose, barely moving her lips.

"Ladies, it is not necessary to provoke unwanted male attention by swinging the hips as you walk," she informed us in her nasal drone. "I will now demonstrate the proper way to walk."

Tucking her buttocks under as far as possible, and throwing her shoulders back, she began walking across the room, holding her arms stiffly at her sides. She looked like both her arms were broken and someone had just poked her in the butt with a broom, but—true to her word —she didn't swing her hips. Even a salty sailor just back from a twelve-month cruise wouldn't have been inspired to whistle as she munched by. More than one girl coughed to hide a snicker, as Miss Beasley launched into her second demonstration.

"And remember, ladies, when sitting in a chair, you do not walk up to the chair and poke your bottom end out." Demonstrating the improper form, Miss Beasley sashayed over to the chair, stopped about three feet in front of it, and poked her bottom out, waving it in one direction, then another, until it finally landed in the chair. Immediately, she jumped up and resumed her buttless stance. "Instead, you back up to the chair and sit slowly, always maintaining your proper, erect posture."

She demonstrated the proper way, looking for all the world like she was teaching patients how to sit after their recent hemorrhoid operations. Fortunately, Etiquette was not a graded course, although we spent several hours practicing the techniques we learned. Of course, most of the practice took place in the barracks at night, amid howls of laughter.

We also had classes on more challenging subjects, such as how to administer first aid in case any of the women injured themselves while walking with their butts tucked into unnatural positions; learning to tell the difference between a guided missile frigate and a destroyer; and memorizing the Navy rank and rating structure. The enlisted ranks were easy. Recruits were at the bottom, followed by apprentices and seamen. Then came the petty officer ranks —third-class, second-class, first-class, and chief. Their insignias were pretty easy to distinguish, but the officer insignias were a little more confusing. Officers had collar and cap insignias, in addition to their sleeve stripes. They had little gold bars, little silver bars, little silver eagles, or little gold oak leaves, depending on their rank—ensign, lieutenant (junior grade), lieutenant commander, commander, or captain. At the top of the structure were several varieties of admirals, such as fleet, vice, and regular.

The most difficult class was Naval Orientation, where we learned new names for old objects and new abbreviations for everything imaginable—the company commander was the CC, the petty officers were POs, the squadron duty officer was the SDO, the military police were the MPs, and so on. And there were involved procedures that made even the simplest tasks become complex assignments. For example, if someone was assigned to stand a fire watch or pick up the mail, she had to report to the squadron duty officer. She couldn't just walk in and give him her best regards. She had to march down to the quarterdeck (quarterdecks are really on ships, but in the Navy they are always pretending buildings are ships, calling the walls "bulkheads" and the stairs "ladders" and stuff). On the quarterdeck, the recruit had to stand at attention on one specific tile of the floor, salute the PO on duty, and request permission to advance to the SDO's office. Once outside the door, she had to stand with the right side of her body touching the doorway and knock with the side of her hand, not moving the rest of her arm. When the SDO answered, she had to request permission to enter his office, salute him, and say she was reporting for duty as ordered. All these things had to be done just exactly right, or they were repeated over and over again. After three tries, if a recruit still couldn't recite all the proper requests and stand in just the right places, she had to take eight hours of special classes in Naval Orientation. The recruit had the choice of taking the classes before breakfast (at four A.M.), at noon (instead of lunch), or during the evening (when everyone else had an hour of free time). If, after completing the special classes, the recruit still couldn't manage to control her feet and mouth well enough to navigate the quarter-deck, she got sent back to a new recruit company and had to start boot camp all over again.

Practicing the procedures in our cubicles was entirely different from doing the actual saluting and reporting. When we had to do the real thing, we panicked. It was like trying to parallel park in a tight space with an official from the Department of Motor Vehicles sitting in the front seat of your car, making notes on a clipboard.

Lucas didn't realize she would have to report to the SDO's office to pick up the mail when she volunteered to be the Mail PO. She told me she only volunteered so that she'd be sure to get any mail from home before the CC saw it. If anyone received a package, PO Pikes made them open it in the lounge and any food had to be shared with the company. Lucas's grandmother had promised to send her some homemade chocolate chip cookies, and she wasn't eager to share them.

"Okay, Johnson," Lucas said. "You be the SDO and I'll practice marching around and knocking on the doors and all that stuff."

"How come you have to practice?" I asked. "Last week

34

when I had to report to the SDO's office before my fire watch, you told me not to worry. You said it was a piece of cake."

"It is," Lucas said.

"So how come you want to practice?" I asked. "You're scared, aren't you?" Lucas was always teasing me for being afraid of the CC and the other officials. She claimed that nobody ever scared her.

"I'm not scared," Lucas insisted. "I just thought you might like to practice. Forget it." She plopped her hat on her head and marched down to the quarterdeck, saluted the duty PO, and advanced to the SDO's office.

When he answered her knock, her voice cracked and her request came out in a mild croak. The SDO screamed, "Louder, Recruit!" That order wasn't in the script as Lucas had memorized and practiced it. She broke into a sweat. Taking a deep breath, she hollered, "Seaman Recruit Lucas, 543-67-9876, Mail Petty Officer, Company 58, requests permission to speak to the SOB!"

When Lucas realized what she had said, she fainted, which was probably the smartest thing she could have done. There must be a rule against punishing unconscious people in basic training, because they carried her and the mail bag up to our company spaces and carefully deposited them both in the CC's office.

3

Chicks Ahoy!

Basic training offers many challenges—learning to stand absolutely still while a stranger screams in your face about the minuscule speck of lint she found on your collar; making your bed so that the blanket overlaps the sheet by *exactly* six inches; getting up at five A.M. every day to go to the gym and do far too many sit-ups and push-ups on a hardwood floor. But the most difficult task our company faced was learning to give up our individuality. Marching around and eating together didn't pose too many problems, but when it came to physical labor such as bed making, it was every woman for herself.

One afternoon, we returned from Etiquette class to find every mattress, sheet, and pillow case torn off the beds and scattered around the room. Pillow cases hung from the bed posts, blankets were piled in the corners, and mattress pads were rolled up in balls and thrown on top of the lockers. Everyone started yelling at once.

"What's going on here?"

"Hey, who screwed up my bunk?"

"What a pigpen!"

Crash! PO Pikes slammed her foot against the trash can. We hadn't noticed her standing in the doorway, with her arms crossed, wearing her familiar I-hate-recruits glare.

36

"You're right, ladies," she said. "This place does look like a pigpen. It looks like a pigpen because there are a lot of selfish pigs in this company. When I inspected your bunks this afternoon, do you know what I found? I found thirty well-made bunks . . . BUT, I found five wrinkled, sloppy racks. That means that thirty of you ladies made your own racks and ignored your company mates who are less accomplished at bunk making."

That's exactly what we had done. I was one of the lucky ones who slept on the top rack. We always made our beds first, standing on the lower bunks in order to reach our beds. The girls with the bottom racks had to smooth out our footprints and then crawl under their racks to pull the covers through the bed springs, without benefit of light or elbow room. It never occurred to me to help someone else make her bed, even though I liked the person. After all, I had shared bunk beds with my sister at home for years and I certainly never had offered to make her bed.

"Maybe you don't think it's important that every bunk be squared away," the CC said as she paced up and down among us, "but if you were in the Fleet—and I doubt if many of you will end up there at this rate—working on an important project, you could cost your company valuable time, equipment, even lives through your inattention to detail. You ladies have got to learn to see the Big Picture. You are not *individuals* anymore. You are now part of a *company* and you had damned well better learn to watch out for your shipmates!"

PO Pikes paused to look at us while we looked at the floor. "You ladies have been here almost nine weeks and you *still* can't march together. You're the only company on base that can't march well enough to earn your company guidon flag. Even the new baby recruits have their guidon. I hope you're proud of yourselves, ladies. I'm certainly not."

After one last look of disgust, the CC spun around and walked out of the room. No one moved. We stood numbly in the center of the room as she called over her shoulder.

"Now get those bunks squared away—and I mean *all* of them—and muster outside for chow in ten minutes."

Ouch! They must have special training classes for company commanders where they teach them how to make recruits feel like dirty little five-year-olds. There wasn't any of the usual chatter as we remade our bunks and the silence continued through dinner and up to Taps.

The next morning, morale picked up a little because we had a rare hour of free time and were authorized to sit in the company lounge and talk and smoke cigarettes and drink sodas and socialize, just like real people. Several girls were sprawled on the chairs and sofas chatting when one girl, Debby Dunbar, suddenly jumped up and wiped her hand on her forearm.

"It's bad enough I have to live in the same cubicle with you, but I don't have to let you touch me, you dirty nigger!" she screamed at the girl who had been sitting beside her, then flounced out of the room.

An uncomfortable hush filled the room. We were all embarrassed by Dunbar's tantrum, but no one knew how to apologize on behalf of the Caucasian race. Helen Nichols was one of the nicest girls in the company, and one of the hardest workers.

"Guess she doesn't know the color doesn't rub off." Helen bravely tried to make a joke to put the rest of us at ease, but her voice cracked in the middle of her sentence and her eyes filled up with tears.

"Excuse me," she whispered and rushed out of the lounge.

Lucas found her voice first. "Geez! That Southern belle makes me sick," she said. "She still thinks she's the prom queen and we're all here to wait on her. I'd rip her lips off, except the CC would probably make me kiss her or something to make up." She stood up and crushed out her cigarette. "I'm going to give Helen a little pep talk. And then I'm going to come up with a plan to take care of Debby Dumbo. You guys wanna help?" The assent was unanimous.

A little while later, Lucas galloped back into the lounge and quickly shut the door.

"Okay, you guys, I got a plan, but you can't breathe a word to anyone. Cross your hearts and hope to spit?" We crossed, although none of us spit.

It was Debby Dunbar's turn to call the commands at our daily drill practice that afternoon. During drill, we marched around the grinder, a cinder-covered parking lot, executing left and right turns and tromping on each other's heels. As individuals, we could each walk at least ten yards without tripping, but in formation we marched like people who had recently purchased new feet and hadn't yet learned to maneuver them.

We spent hours practicing in the barracks, and frequently marched each other into walls before we could remember the command that would turn the group around. On the grinder, we took turns guiding the group by running alongside the company, shouting directions. The recruit giving the orders received her grade based on how authoritative she sounded and how well the company followed her commands.

"Ah-ten-HUT!" Dunbar hollered. We all fell into line at attention, waiting for the order to begin marching.

"Forward, harch!" (For some unknown reason, the

39

Navy teaches recruits to pronounce "march" with an "h." PO Pikes said she didn't know why, it had always been done it that way. I figured the person who typed the first drill manual made a typo and wrote "harch" instead of "march" and by the time the big brass finally noticed it, people had been harching for years and it was too late to change it. Everything has to be uniform in the military, and if one person goes around saying "harch" then everyone has to do it.)

We all stepped forward in unison and Dunbar looked smug. Her voice grew more confident as she issued her next command.

"By the right flank, harch!" Lucas and I turned left, most of the company turned right, and six or seven girls turned and marched to the rear. Dunbar started screaming, "Stop! No, no—I mean, Company, halt! Stop!"

We froze in place. It looked like a game of freeze tag. PO Pikes's face showed no expression as she stood watching from the far side of the grinder. She was close enough to see clearly, but not to hear the commands.

"Ah-ten-HUT!" Dunbar looked confused as we lined up again.

"Forward, harch!"

Again, we marched forward.

"By the right flank, harch!" This time, three of us stopped marching, three continued forward, four turned around to the rear, and the rest turned to the left or right.

Dunbar glanced over at PO Pikes, who was calmly tapping her pencil against the top of her clipboard.

"Ah-ten-HUT!" Dunbar screeched.

"Don't you dare screw it up again, you mean things!" she whispered as we scurried into our places.

"Dress right, dress!" Each girl was supposed to put her right hand on her hip and turn her head to the right, making sure the line she stood in was exactly straight. The girls at the right end of the line were supposed to look forward and serve as the guides.

When Dunbar gave the command to "dress right," heads turned in all directions and half of us put our left arms out straight in front of us.

"I hate you creeps!" Dunbar stamped her foot and pouted. "Why won't you all do this right?"

"Maybe we can't hear what you're saying because your mouth is filled with dirty words like 'nigger,' " came a voice from the rear.

"Oh, shit!" Dunbar shrugged her shoulders in defeat as PO Pikes approached. She couldn't complain about us without stepping on her own tail.

"Seems like you have a little problem here, Dunbar," said the CC, as she made another notation on her checklist. "Let's see if you can do a little better, Lucas."

Lucas put us through our paces and the company executed each command perfectly. PO Pikes shook her head in disbelief.

"I thought maybe the company was messing up, Dunbar. But it doesn't seem to be that way. Looks like you are the one who needs practice."

Dunbar opened her mouth to protest, but reconsidered when she saw the glaring faces surrounding her. She sighed loudly, but didn't say anything.

"Don't worry about it, Dunbar," said the CC. "I'll make sure you get a few hours of extra practice calling commands out here on the drill field."

That night, Dunbar walked into the lounge, where most of the company was gathered, discussing the day's events. Not a glance or a greeting acknowledged her presence.

"Listen," she said to the group. "I know you're all

mad at me, but you have to understand that I grew up in Alabama and we just don't associate with colored people."

"We don't have to understand shit," Lucas stood up. "You're the one who has to understand. We're all in this company, whether we like it or not. And we have to work together to get out of this place. We don't need some spoiled brat running around causing problems. This company could get along just fine without you, but you can't graduate from basic training without our help. Don't you understand that?" Lucas was an inspirational speaker when she got fired up.

Dunbar shrugged her shoulders. "Yeah, I guess so."

"Okay, then shut up and sit down." Lucas slapped Dunbar on the back. "Actually, you did the company a favor, in a strange kind of way. Did you see how we pulled together as a team out there on the drill field?"

"Yeah, I saw you," Dunbar pouted. "But *I* wasn't part of the team."

"Well, I bet you could be on our team," Lucas said, "if you apologize to Nichols and start acting like a human being. What do you say, Dunbar?"

"Aw, come on—" Dunbar started to argue, but she glanced around the room at the unfriendly faces and shrugged. "Okay, I guess I really don't have much choice, do I? But it won't be easy," she mumbled.

Lucas crossed her arms over her chest and strutted around the room in a darned good imitation of PO Pikes. "This is boot camp, recruit! Did you think this was summer camp?" She stalked up to Dunbar. "If you want to be in my Navy, recruit, if you want to wear The Blue, then you can't go around calling people niggers. Is that understood?" she cried.

"Yes, ma'am!" Dunbar saluted, spun on her heels, and

marched out of the lounge toward the cube where Nichols sat reading a book.

"Hurry up and get back in here so you can see the nifty report card me and my pal Johnson drew up," Lucas called after her.

As we neared the end of our training, we were feeling pretty cocky, so Lucas and I decided to make a report card to send to our parents so they could see what we'd been learning these past weeks when we had so little time or energy to write letters home. On a piece of white cardboard, we'd written:

Basic Training Report Card

Subject	Grade	Comments
Mustering	A	Possesses the required two arms
Standing at attention	B	Occasionally farts during inspections
Stowing Lockers	C	Pantie folds aren't straight, tsk tsk!
Speed Eating	A	Eats faster than a speeding bullet
Cleaning Toilets	A	Really puts her heart (and hand) in it
Singing Ditties	B	Sings off-key, but real loud
Writing name on things	A+	Handles a Magic Marker like a pro
Etiquette	D	Swings hips like shameless hussy
Crispy Shirts	A	Crinkles when she moves
Deck Swabbing	A	Popeye would be proud

43

Your daughter is the best darned recruit I have ever had the pleasure of training. She is intelligent, hard-working, responsible, and extremely generous to the other women in her company. She still has a few problems folding her underwear into neat little squares and walking with her butt tucked under, but she does have wonderful posture and is a champion speed eater. Thanks ever so much for sending her to the Navy and if you have any more at home like her, why not send them along, too?

PO Pikes
Company Commander

I stood up in front of the group and read the report card, pausing occasionally to remind the girls to keep their laughter down because PO Pikes was in her office around the corner.

"I love it!" Dunbar said.

"I bet PO Pikes would love it, too!" I joked. "Any volunteers to show it to her?"

"Show me what?" I couldn't believe it! PO Pikes was leaning against the doorway of the lounge with her arms crossed, tapping one foot on the floor.

"Oh, it's nothing," I said. "Just a funny little letter we're working on to send to our parents. We're not done with it yet, but we'll show it to you tomorrow, if you'd like to see it." I could feel a little trickle of sweat running down the side of my forehead as I spoke.

The CC wasn't easily dissuaded. "I don't mind seeing the unfinished version," she insisted. "Bring that paper over here, Johnson."

I looked at the paper and then at Lucas. "Think I should eat it, Lucas?" I whispered. I considered the idea for a

44

moment, but realized it wouldn't help. They'd probably pump my stomach. Lucas apparently reached the same conclusion. She shook her head and crossed herself, even though I had told her a hundred times that I had personal proof that God wasn't allowed to help recruits.

"I said bring that paper over here, recruit," PO Pikes said in her don't-argue-with-me voice. I jumped up and handed PO Pikes the report card. My hand was shaking so hard that the paper rattled.

Everyone in the room held her breath as she silently read the card. As she read, the muscles in the side of her jaws began twitching. I'd seen that twitch before. My dad's jaws always twitched when he was trying hard to control either his anger or his laughter.

Finally, PO Pikes looked up, but didn't say a word. She rubbed her chin and looked at the ceiling. Then she drummed the fingers of her left hand against her right forearm, obviously trying to decide what to do with us.

"Well, ladies, I don't want you to think that your company commander has no sense of humor," she said. "This report card is actually quite funny."

Lucas heaved a huge sigh and quickly crossed herself again. I said a silent "thank you" of my own, happy to know that the prayer lines between Orlando and Heaven had been reconnected. But I had prayed too soon.

"On the other hand," the CC continued, "I don't want you to think that it is acceptable, under any circumstances, to be disrespectful to a military superior, even if he or she is not in your presence. You ladies may have completed nine weeks of training, but you still have another week to go. It's still not too late for you to earn twenty demerits and be recycled to a brand new company. Is that understood?"

"*Yes, ma'am!*" we chorused.

"Good. Now, I have a little project to entertain you this evening."

We groaned in unison; we were all familiar with the CC's little projects.

"I have some old toothbrushes in my office and I hate to throw them away while they still have bristles left on them. So, why don't you ladies use those toothbrushes to strip and wax the barracks floor?"

"Oh, God!"

"You have to be kidding!"

"Do I look like I'm kidding?" barked the CC, resuming her familiar gruff expression. She most certainly didn't.

"I'm not sure who wrote this report card," the CC added, "but I have a good idea. So, you ladies make the choice. You can either strip and wax the floor together, or the person who wrote this card can do it herself. It's up to you. Either way, it had better be done by 0500, even if it takes all night."

Lucas and I looked at each other, nodded, and quickly stood up, but before we could open our mouths to claim authorship, the other girls all jumped up.

"We'll all do it," Dunbar said. "We're a company." A couple of girls snickered, noticing the change in Dunbar's attitude. Just a few hours ago, she would have been the first to complain if she had to help someone else. PO Pikes looked amused, too.

"I'm glad you said that." The CC actually smiled at us! "If you ladies had deserted one of your shipmates, I would have given you all twenty demerits because it would have meant I had failed to teach you the essence of teamwork. I'd have had to send you to another company commander to see if she could teach you where I had failed."

Those words were as close to praise as we ever got from PO Pikes. We were so thrilled that we almost had fun

46

working on the floor. We sang all the songs we knew and made up a few more of our own. Singing helped us keep our minds off our aching knees as we crawled around, scrubbing every single speck of wax off the tile. After about four hours, we heard a clanking sound near the head. One of the girls went to investigate the noise and found a bottle of heavy-duty ammonia detergent sitting beside a pail of brushes and mops outside the head. The CC never did anything by accident, so we realized that it was her way of letting us off the hook without appearing to be softhearted.

Muster was slow the next morning, because most of us kept stopping to rub our stiff knees. Grumbling and mumbling, we lined up on the sidewalk in the cool morning air. We were so sleepy that it took a few minutes before anyone noticed PO Pikes standing in front of the barracks— holding our company guidon flag! Suddenly, everyone stood a little straighter. We knew we had truly earned that flag. PO Pikes would have made us go all the way through graduation without a flag before she'd have given us an award that we hadn't fairly earned.

During the rest of our tenth week, there wasn't much time to get in trouble. We were too busy taking final exams and filling out requests for duty assignments. A bulletin board hanging just outside the lounge displayed our grades and duty assignments. Luckily, everyone passed the finals, but quite a few people received different duty assignments than the ones their recruiters had guaranteed.

My recruiter had given me a card with her signature, guaranteeing me a seat in the next journalism class. She told me to hide the card when I got to basic training and wait until I got my orders. If I didn't get orders to school,

I was to call my recruiting office and show the card to my CC. Supposedly, if I didn't get to go to journalism school, my contract would be void and I would be a free, independent civilian again.

Most of the assignments were already posted and I was beginning to get nervous. For ten weeks, I had done nothing but complain, along with the rest of my company, about how horrible the Navy was and how much we hated it and wanted to go back home. But, to my surprise, when I really considered going back home, I realized how much I wanted to stay in the Navy. Basic training was an adventure of sorts, but I hadn't had any real exciting escapades or done any traveling yet.

My name finally showed up on the list, with an assignment to journalism training at Defense Information School (DINFOS), Fort Benjamin Harrison, Indiana. I was surprised to see that Lucas was also going to DINFOS.

"Hey, Lucas, why didn't you tell me you were going to JO school, too?" I asked her.

"Well, Johnson," she said, "you're such a pain in the ass, I wasn't sure I wanted to go to the same school with you." The look on my face must have made Lucas realize that I believed her.

"I was only kidding, Johnson." She chuckled and patted me on the head. "You're so gullible. It's a good thing I'm going to JO school so I can keep an eye on you. You'd never make it without me." She punched me lightly on the arm. "Now, let's go get ready for inspection. Lucky for you, we get to wear our high heels today. You won't have to spend half an hour trying to tie your shoes!"

"You're *so* witty, Lucas."

"I know, Johnson," she smirked. "That's why they let *me* into journalism school without a note from my recruiter."

For our final inspection, we were authorized to wear our blue dress uniforms for the first time, which was a stroke of psychological brilliance. If the CC had told us that we had to wear fully lined wool suits and stand out in the ninety-eight-degree sun the first day we had arrived in Orlando, I'm sure that the girls in our company would have realized immediately that we were in the presence of a dangerously insane person. No doubt we all would have turned around and climbed right back on the bus and gone home, contracts or no contracts.

Since none of us had had the foresight to get back on the bus, we had spent every day for nearly ten weeks wearing orthopedic shoes, one-size-fits-all-including-thunder-thighs trousers, baggy blue shirts that each had room for a healthy female chest plus three or four watermelons, and wool hats that draped over our heads like blue banana peels. After that experience, the opportunity to wear nylon stockings, high-heeled shoes, and skirts was pretty darned exciting, even if it was a hot, humid July afternoon in Florida.

A female Navy commander was coming to inspect our company and PO Pikes made it very clear that anyone who didn't pass inspection wouldn't graduate from basic training. You'd have thought we were going to the prom, the way we primped and prettied ourselves for that inspection. After we dressed, we took turns brushing each other several times with our lint brushes. No matter how hard we tried, the CC always managed to find lint, dirt specks, and stray hairs on our uniforms. I secretly believed that she carried a small supply of dirt and lint in her pocket and unobtrusively placed them in strategic spots during inspections, but I kept my suspicions to myself. She seemed to get so much pleasure out of marking things down on her clipboard. I couldn't see the point in spoiling her fun. Besides, I knew she'd find a "little project" to occupy me for about the next ten years if I blew her cover.

Certified as lint-free, I put on my black pumps. I had spent hours polishing them to a glossy shine and could actually see the reflection of my teeth in the toes. Of course, I couldn't see my teeth while I was wearing them. I had to hold them up in front of my face to do that. Since I usually wore my shoes on my feet, I realized, much too late, that I would rarely have a chance to display my spit-shining expertise.

"Would you quit admiring your dental work and help me put this dumb hat on straight?" Lucas was standing in the middle of the cube, with her hat on sideways. When I looked up, she tucked her butt under and minced across the room, just as our Etiquette teacher, Miss Beasley, had instructed. Her demonstration was interrupted by the call to muster outside. I quickly turned her hat so the silver anchor insignia faced forward and we headed for the stairs to join the other girls. Usually, we screamed down the stairs in a noisy herd, but that afternoon we walked slowly, with our shoulders back and our heads high. Hey, this was no time to mess around. We were wearing The Blue.

We were the last of six companies to be inspected, so we had to stand outside, baking in the sunlight, for over an hour, waiting for the inspecting officer to arrive. The CC knew we'd never be able to stand still for that long, so she let us stand at parade rest, which meant we could spread our feet about a foot and a half apart, but we still had to stand with our arms motionless, hands clasped in the middle of our lower backs.

The spray starch in my shirt melted because of the heat and I could feel it dripping slowly down between my shoulder blades. I was trying to decide if I wanted to pass the inspection more than I wanted to scratch my back, when the inspecting officer finally showed up. The CC called the company to attention, which put scratching out of the question. The CC and the captain took their time moving down the line, and the itch was getting worse by the second, so I decided to use self-hypnosis to control the itching. I rolled my eyes up into my head and took deep breaths as I whispered "It doesn't itch. It doesn't itch" under my breath. Within a few minutes, the itching began to numb —but so did everything else—and I passed out cold.

When I came to, the CC was holding my head, gently slapping my face.

"How many times have I told you not to lock your knees when you're standing at attention, Johnson?" she asked.

"Did I flunk? Did I flunk?" I had to know.

"You passed, Johnson," the CC said. "You fell over at attention and stayed that way!"

The CC wanted to send me to the dispensary, but I begged her to let me stay with the company for the march around the drill field. I didn't want to miss the graduation parade.

"Please, PO Pikes," I pleaded. "I've been working for ten weeks and I finally get to wear The Blue. I promise not to pass out again."

"Okay, Johnson," she agreed, "but if you do, I'm going to keep you in my company for another ten weeks. Do you still want to march in the parade?"

"Yes, ma'am." I saluted and ran off to join the company before she had a chance to change her mind.

A Navy band was playing "Anchors Aweigh" as the families and friends of the recruits took their seats on bleachers that had been placed at the edge of the drill field. The color guard marched into place and everyone stood up for the national anthem. The civilians covered their hearts

51

and the military people all faced the flag and saluted. Swords and medals flashed in the sun and the music swelled up around us.

My heart felt so big as I stood saluting the flag, my fingers barely touching the brim of my hat. I was in the back row, so I could see all my shipmates standing straight and proud in their dress uniforms, with the flag waving against the blue sky in the background.

When the music ended, the commanding officer of the base made a speech about how proud he was that we had met the challenges of basic training head on and how he was proud to have us in the Navy. Then we began the big march around the grinder, each company displaying its guidon. As we passed the reviewing stand where the commanding officer stood, the CC called "Eyes, right!" and we all snapped our heads to the right as our feet kept marching forward.

We followed our feet off the field and directly to the barracks to pick up the luggage that we had packed the night before. A few people changed into civilian clothes, which now looked strange and rather wrinkled to us, after seeing only uniforms for nearly three months. We all rushed in and grabbed our bags, but no one rushed out the door. We were reluctant to leave these young women with whom we had shared so much of our lives in such a short period of time. Instinctively, we knew that with a few exceptions, we would never see each other again.

"I have one more little project for you ladies before you leave!" The CC had to yell in order to be heard above the hubbub.

"*Oh, no!*"

"*Spare me!*"

"I think you'll like this project," the CC said. "I'd like

you to sing your company song one more time before you leave."

No one argued. We loved our company song. The CC had taught us the first verse, but we wrote the second one ourselves. She started singing and we all joined in:

If they could see me now, that little gang of mine,
I'm eating Navy chow and telling Navy time.
I wish those guys back home could see for a fact
The kind of first-rate girls the Navy attracts.
All I can say is, "Wowee, look at where I am!
I'm dressed in Navy blue and work for Uncle Sam."
There's such a change in their old pal, they'd never
    believe it
If my friends could see me now!

If they could see me now, they'd really flip their lids.
They wouldn't recognize this former sloppy kid.
They'd see me ironing shirts and shining my shoes.
The hometown newspaper would print the big news.
They'd say, "Our local girl is now a sailorette,
You'll find her standing watch and even swabbing
    decks."
There's such a change in this old girl—they'd never
    believe it
If my friends could see me now!

"Thank you, ladies," the CC said as soon as we sang the last note. "You're in my Navy now, so do me proud." She clapped her hands and put on her official face. "Now, you have five seconds to get out of my barracks or I'll sign you up for another ten weeks."

There was a wild stampede for the door, where parents stood peering cautiously inside, curious to see where their precious babies had been living. I glanced back at the CC just before I went out the door.

She stood at parade rest in the middle of the empty barracks, watching her latest crop of recruits head out to the Fleet. I could have sworn I saw a tear glistening in her eye, but it was probably just the light reflecting off one of the bare metal bunks.

4

Best
Pals

"Good morning, ladies!" *(Clash!)*

I opened one eye just wide enough to see First Sergeant Burke standing in the center of the room, holding a metal trash can lid in each hand. She punctuated her sentences by clanging the lids together.

"Let's get a move on!" *(Clash!)* "I want to see your ugly mugs in my office in exactly two minutes. *(Clash!)*"

I opened the other eye and looked at the clock. Only five A.M., and none of my roommates was moving yet, so I stayed in my bunk. But Sergeant Burke wasn't a patient woman. She was short, skinny, ugly, and cruel to the enlisted women who lived in the barracks under her charge.

"I'm waiting, ladies!" *(Clash!)* "I don't like to wait. Waiting makes me nervous." *(Clash!)* "When I get nervous, I have to call a barracks inspection." *(Clash! Clash! Clash!)*

In less than a minute, my seven roommates and I were on our feet, slamming open our metal lockers, grabbing blouses, neckties, slacks, and black leather oxfords. The last one out of bed, as usual, was Lucas. She groaned as she rolled from her rack beneath mine to the floor.

"What's up?" Lucas hadn't changed a bit since boot camp. She was always the last one into bed at night and the last one dressed in the morning. This morning was no exception. Our loyal roommates were already well on their way to Sgt. Burke's office, so I tied Lucas's shoes while she buttoned her blouse and we ran to catch up with the group.

"What time is it, pal?" Lucas asked. "Seems like I just went to sleep." She hadn't had time to dig her watch out of the pile of clothing on the bottom of her locker.

I stabbed Lucas in the arm with my finger. "You *did* just go to sleep, pal! You woke me up when you staggered in at four A.M., singing one of your original, but extremely dumb, songs."

Lucas was one of those people who do their best sleeping during daylight hours. She could sleep while standing at attention, but put her in a bunk in the dark and she was wide awake. She spent most nights at the enlisted club, playing cards with the bartender. Lucas drank a few beers once in a while, but she hardly ever got really drunk. Everyone thought she was a drunk, though, because she spent so much time at the club. I liked to pretend I thought so, too, because it made her mad.

Sergeant Burke scowled at us from the doorway of her office. "Get a move on, you two!" she hollered. Inside, the top of her usually immaculate desk was covered with little glass bottles. She crossed her arms and nodded her head towards the bottles.

"Okay, ladies," Sgt. Burke said. "Fill one up and then get your lazy butts outta here."

"Whaddya want us to fill them with, Sarge? Watah?" Lucas asked, stressing her New England accent. She got a real kick out of giving Sgt. B. a hard time. I liked to hassle the sarge, too, but we had to live in her barracks for another two months until we finished school. So far, we'd been there three weeks and we'd both pulled extra guard duty every weekend.

PO Pikes had promised that life would be different after

basic training. There wouldn't be four girls living in a tiny cubicle, she said, and there wouldn't be so much emphasis placed on waxing and buffing gray tile floors. As usual, PO Pikes was right. In the Army, there were *eight* girls living in the same room and there are acres of *green* tile floors to wax and buff. People from all the services attended the same journalism school, which was located on an Army base, so the Waves had to live with the Army Wacs in the barracks run by Sgt. Burke. Sgt. Burke hated Waves. Actually, she hated everyone, but she particularly hated Waves.

"I want you to fill these bottles with urine, ladies," Sgt. Burke sneered. "I thought you'd be smart enough to figure that out." She snapped her fingers. "Darn! I forgot you two are in the Navy. In your case, I shoulda said, 'Do your pee-pee in da bottle.' "

A Navy person on an Army base has to expect to take a little good-natured ribbing from the Army troops, but Sergeant Burke turned every encounter into a major battle and she didn't hesitate to call in reinforcements. She took great delight in making Waves follow orders that she knew would cause repercussions from Navy superiors. Once she ordered us to wear the wrong hats with our uniforms. She even followed us to school to make sure we didn't change them. When my instructor asked why I wasn't wearing the proper uniform, I told him Sgt. Burke ordered me to wear the hat. She denied it, of course, and claimed that I was lying, just to cause trouble. Then she gave me eight hours of extra guard duty for telling on her. I also got demerits in school for wearing an improper uniform and acting disrespectfully to a senior noncommissioned officer.

Eager to avoid another such incident, I grabbed Lucas's arm and pushed her in the direction of the bathroom before she could open her mouth again. There was no point in arguing with Sgt. Burke.

"Come on, Lucas, just pee in the bottle so we can get to school," I whispered. "The Sarge isn't fully equipped for mental combat with a genius like you and you'll end up cleaning the barracks tonight if you prove it to her." I pulled Lucas out of Sgt. Burke's office.

"Okay, pal," Lucas said. "But I don't see why we gotta pee in these little bottles."

"Neither do I. Maybe they're doing some experiments to find out why us Waves are so much better looking than these Wacs!"

"Ha!" Lucas chortled. "That's it, pal! Geez, but you're smart. No wonder you like me so much."

I filled my bottle and returned to Sgt. Burke's office. She was filling out forms and wrapping them around the bottles, taking great care to separate the Army urine from the Navy urine. I could just imagine the breach in national security if the samples got confused and the medical corpsmen couldn't tell whose urine was which.

"What's this for, Sergeant B.?" I had to ask. My curiosity was stronger than my distaste for conversation with Sgt. Burke.

She carefully attached a label to one of the bottle. "We're checking you scumbags for drugs, Johnson," she said. "Drugs and booze show up in your urine, in case you didn't know."

I asked whether one or two beers would show up or if you had to drink a lot.

"You writin' a book?" Sgt. Burke was a master of the unoriginal retort. "Don't worry about how much you can drink. You oughta be worried about your drunk friend." She leaned back in her chair and rubbed her palms together. "If I can prove she's a drinker, she'll get sent to

58

alcohol rehab or maybe even kicked out of the service."

I *was* worried. I knew Lucas had been drunk last night. She only wrote dumb songs on the rare occasions when she was drunk. But I knew she wasn't an alcoholic. No one would believe it though, because I was her best friend and I was always calling her a drunk just because I liked to hear her holler.

Lucas brought her bottle into the office and set it down ever so carefully on Sgt. Burke's desk, beside a large brass eagle which was the only decoration in the office, except for a large portrait of the President, our Commander-in-Chief and Sgt. Burke's idol. I couldn't figure out why Lucas was grinning at me as we left the office. I didn't think the situation was very humorous.

"Don't look so worried," Lucas whispered as we walked out the door. "I do my best thinking in the can. I figured it was a trap. I had a few beers last night, so I filled my bottle halfway and then added some water." She patted herself on the head, proud of her ingenuity.

"Hold it, you worms!" screamed Sgt. Burke.

Lucas didn't even turn around. She just grabbed my arm and dragged me down the hallway. "Sorry, Sarge," Lucas called over her shoulder. "We gotta get to school."

"You'll pay for this, you scum! Mark my words." I managed to turn around for one final look as Lucas pulled me out the front door. Sgt. Burke was wiping her hands with a paper towel and muttering to herself. Lucas had filled her bottle to the very brim so that some of the urine spilled onto Sgt. B.'s hand when she picked up the bottle to wrap the label around it. I laughed for about ten seconds—until I realized we'd have to pay for that little joke.

Lucas insisted that Sgt. Burke was going to give us extra duties anyway, so we might as well enjoy ourselves.

I reminded her that everything we did at school would show up on our permanent records.

"Relax, pal," Lucas said. "You're such a lifer."

"I am not!" I knew she was just paying me back for calling her a drunk, but I hated to be called a lifer. "I joined the Navy so I could travel and get an education, not because I couldn't get a job. I'm not a lifer!"

"Yes you are, pal. You're a lifer," Lucas said with a mischievous grin. She knew she was getting to me. "And you know what that stands for—a 'Lazy Ignorant Fucker Expecting Retirement.' "

I shook my fist in Lucas's face. "You're really making me mad," I fumed. "Let's change the subject while we're still pals, okay?"

"Okay by me, pal," Lucas agreed. She was silent for about five seconds, then muttered, "But I like you even if you are a lifer!" and ran ahead so I couldn't smack her.

"Lucas!" I yelled. "I owe you one for that. Consider yourself warned. *I'll get you.*"

Sometimes Lucas really pissed me off, but she was the best pal I ever had. If it weren't for her, I'd still be back in boot camp, trying to learn to iron a shirt. Of course, without me, she'd still be in boot camp trying to learn to shine her shoes. By pooling our resources, we had managed to convince PO Pikes that we could be trusted to dress ourselves in the proper Navy style. We didn't have daily inspections at Fort Ben, but we still had to look spiffy because all the journalism instructors were senior Navy petty officers or Army officers. I still shined our shoes, but Lucas sent the shirts out to the laundry. The laundry didn't iron shirts as well as Lucas did, but she preferred to take life easy whenever possible.

Unfortunately, Sgt. Burke didn't share Lucas's philosophy. The good sergeant was afraid we'd get soft if we didn't spend two or three hours a day on our knees, scrubbing toilets or guarding the barracks against the hordes of communist spies who lurked outside waiting for a chance to sneak in and steal our plans for dusting the tops of our lockers and keeping the metal knobs on the drinking fountains shiny. Lucas and I shared a room with six Wacs who were all attending the Finance school on base, so we didn't see much of our roommates, except when we cleaned our room.

Every evening, a chart was posted in the hallway that listed the cleaning details for the next day. In the morning, the room had to be spotless before we left for school. As soon as the reveille bugle sounded, the cleaning squads went into action. One girl dusted the tops of the lockers and desks, another girl followed with a broom and dustpan, while a third emptied the trash. The next assault was the mop and wax squad. Finally, two girls would drag in a large electric buffer and attempt to polish the floor to a glossy military shine. The buffers in our barracks were very old and so heavy that it took two people to handle one buffer. If one person tried to run the buffer, it would rise up off the floor and head for the nearest wall, where it would sit buffing and humming contently in the same spot until it was turned off. In an attempt to weight the buffer down so it could be guided around the floor, one girl sat on top of the buffer while another operated the controls. Our method didn't stop the buffer from heading for the wall, but it slowed it down enough that we could usually buff a few tiles in the center of the room on the way to the wall. If we got done in time, we would all skate around the middle of the floor in our socks to shine it up a little bit. The inspecting officers were familiar with the buffer action, so they were usually satisfied if the corners of the room were shiny, with a few streaks of gloss across the rest of the floor—proof that the troops had made a valiant effort to buff before heading out to the chow hall for breakfast on the way to school.

Military training schools teach the same subjects as civilian ones, but there were some differences that I noticed right away. Instead of a dean's list to reward the students with good grades, military schools give them assignments to nice duty stations like Hawaii or Paris and the very best students are sometimes promoted to a higher rank. On the other hand, if you don't do your homework in a civilian school, you flunk. Military students don't flunk; they get "recycled" until they either give up and learn the material or are given assignments to the North Pole, where they will have plenty of free time to ponder the merits of scholarship while slowly freezing to death.

Thanks to Sergeant Burke's dislike for Waves, my grades were good enough to put me in the top ten percent of the class after the first month of classes. Since I had spent my first three weekends on guard duty, where I was only allowed to read military manuals to amuse myself, I had read most of my textbooks ahead of the class schedule. I planned to keep my grades high enough to qualify for my choice of duty stations so I could request orders to the Philippine islands. The Philippines are thirteen thousand miles away from Youngsville, Pennsylvania, about as far away as I could travel yet still be on the same planet.

The weekend after the urine tests, neither Lucas nor I was assigned weekend guard duty, so we were dumb enough to think Sgt. Burke had forgotten all about the incidents. Monday morning, she issued a correction to the guard schedule. We both had *double duty* the night before one of our biggest tests. That meant two eight-hour watches, back to back, and we had to go straight to school after the second watch. I knew I'd be so tired that I'd flunk my exams.

I decided to see the senior Navy man on the base to ask if he could intervene on our behalf. Chief Petty Officer Hatch was a big man, with a good-sized beer belly. When I finished my story, he snorted, hitched up his pants, set his coffee cup down amid the papers scattered over his desk, and pulled a pack of cigarettes out of his sock. He bit the filter off a cigarette, touched the end of it to his tongue, and put it in his mouth. Then he pulled out a match book, bent a match, and lit it with one hand. He took a couple of puffs before he answered me.

"Your first sergeant already called me, Johnson," he said. He kept his cigarette in the corner of his mouth while he talked, so the smoke drifted up into his face, making him squint.

"Seems you and your buddy haven't been too cooperative over at the barracks. Sergeant Burke has a big job over there. She also has some high-ranking Army friends on this base, if you know what I mean."

I realized that he wasn't going to be able to help us, so I thanked him and got up to leave his office. Just as I was about to walk out the door, he called me back inside.

"Sit down," he said, nodding to the chair in front of his desk. "I might be able to do something for you, if you were willing to do a little favor for me."

"What's that, Chief?" I figured he had some typing to do or some other administrative chores. I handled a typewriter about as well as I handled an iron, but I could always get Lucas to help.

"Well, uh, it's not official business." He scratched his forearm, pulling up his sleeve to reveal a tattoo of a naked lady. She had a big snake wound around her legs, with its head between her gigantic breasts. When he noticed me

63

staring at it, he licked his lips and leered at me. That's when I realized that there wasn't going to be a typewriter involved in his little favor. I stood up and grabbed my books off his desk.

"Don't get all excited, now, sweetheart," Chief Hatch laughed. "With an ass like yours, you'll get good grades. And don't be surprised if you get offers to do a few extra 'assignments' for promotion, too. You'd better get used to it, because this is a man's Navy, whether you like it or not."

By the time I walked the half-mile back to the barracks, I had calmed down a little, but when I told Lucas about my conversation with Chief Hatch, I got mad all over again.

"How could he talk to me like that?" I fumed.

"He can talk to you any way he wants to, 'cause he's a chief," she said. "What are you gonna do about it, anyway? Tell some admiral that a sailor talked dirty to you?" Lucas wasn't very sympathetic.

"Maybe I will." The idea held some appeal.

"Sure, pal. Who do you think he's gonna believe—a peon like you or a chief petty officer with twenty years in the Navy?" Lucas tapped her finger against her temple. "Sometimes you're so dumb I can't believe it. I know you were raised out in the hills of Pennsylvania somewhere, but didn't they teach you anything?"

"I'll show that creep!" I fumed, ignoring her comments about my upbringing. "I'll study hard and get the best grades and then I'll be the honor graduate and he'll have to admit that some women get promoted because they work hard, not because of how they use their bodies!"

Lucas snickered and shook her head. "I really doubt you'll ever get Chief Big Belly to admit anything, Johnson.

64

He'll probably just order somebody to flunk you so he can laugh at you."

I whirled around, astonished at such a thought. "He couldn't do that!"

"Well, he probably won't, but I bet he could if he wanted to," Lucas said.

"It's just not fair!" I slammed my locker door against the wall and threw my books in the bottom.

Lucas stretched out on her bunk, crossed her hands behind her head, and sighed loudly.

"How many times do I have to tell you, pal?" she asked. "There ain't no Navy regulation that says life has to be fair. You just have to learn to accept the fact that this is a man's Navy. Talking dirty to women is one of their requirements for promotion."

"I'll show him a promotion!" I kicked the side of my metal locker, which produced a satisfying clang. "I'll get such good grades that they have to promote me or I'll write a letter to the President. That's what I'll do!" I was really charged up.

"Settle down," Lucas said. "You've been fuming and pacing around here for an hour."

"You're absoluely right!" I said. "I could have spent this time studying. Where are my books?" I dug frantically in the bottom of my locker, pulling out the books that I had thrown in a pile. I carried them to the desk and spread them out, but I had trouble concentrating because I was so mad. Every few minutes, I'd stop and mutter, "Ha! I'll show him who has to use her ass to get promoted!"

"Eeeek!"

Lucas had walked up behind me and put her hand on my shoulder, but I'd been so absorbed in my thoughts that, startled, I jumped out of my chair, tripped, and fell on the floor.

"Come on." Lucas pulled me to my feet. "You can't study when you're so tense. Let's go over to the club. You need to relax, play some cards, tell a few jokes about chauvinistic men."

"You know any good jokes about fat, stupid chiefs?" I asked as she pulled me out the door.

At the club, I was so involved in playing gin rummy and complaining about Chief Hatch that I didn't even realize I had been drinking the beer the bartender put on the table. By the time I noticed what I'd been doing, Lucas and I had emptied a large pitcher, so she was feeling a little shaky herself. Neither one of us could walk very well, so we decided to crawl back to the barracks. Progress was slow, because we had to stop frequently and slap each other on the back while we laughed at our hilarious jokes.

"Hey, pal," I said. "Next time I see a sailor, I'm gonna say, 'Are you happy to see me or is that a pencil in your pocket?' "

We laughed so hard at that one that we both fell down in the road, which felt pretty comfortable. We were lying flat on our stomachs, giggling, when I noticed four shiny boots in front of my face. I looked up a little higher and saw two military policemen attached to the boots.

"Looks like you ladies have had a little too much to drink tonight, haven't you?" asked the one who was shining a flashlight on us.

"No, we didn't get *enough*," Lucas screamed. "We can still see!"

It occurred to me that the MPs might not appreciate our humor, but I couldn't stop laughing.

"Okay," said the flashlight holder. "We oughta write you ladies up for this, but we're gonna be nice guys this time. Besides, Lucas is a good buddy of mine. I owe her thirty-five bucks for whipping my butt in our last gin rummy game." He put his hands under my elbows and pulled me to his feet while his partner picked Lucas up. "We're gonna put you in the truck and drive you to the barracks. In your condition, you're major road hazards."

"Thank you very mush," Lucas slurred. "You're gentlemen and I'm sorry for what my pal said about your penshils."

"What pencils?" the MP asked.

Lucas started to point to his crotch, but I punched her in the head. "She's delirious, sir," I said. "She doesn't know what she's saying." Fortunately, Lucas fell asleep until we reached the baracks.

Once inside, we crawled down the hallway towards our room. We had waxed and buffed the green tile floor so often that it gleamed in the moonlight.

"Let's be real quiet, pal," Lucas said, "or we'll wake up Sgt. Burke and she'll come out and make us pee in a bottle. Then I'll have to go to drug rehabilitation and you'll never get to be an admiral."

"Shh!" I put my finger to my lips, which made me lose my balance and I banged into the wall. "You're screaming, Lucas."

"I am not!" she screamed.

Lucas slept in the bunk under me. It was our custom to whisper, "G'night, pal," before going to sleep each night. But I hadn't forgotten her insults about me being a lifer. I decided not to say, "G'night."

"G'night, pal," Lucas whispered.

I didn't answer.

"G'night, pal." A little louder now. Lucas kicked the bottom of my mattress, making the bed springs squeak. The girl in the next bunk turned over and mumbled.

"G'night, pal!" Lucas was getting upset and I was trying hard not to laugh.

"G'night, pal!" she hollered.

"Shut your fat mouth, Lucas! I'll come over there and give you a 'g'night pal' punch in the face in about two minutes if you don't shut up!"

The Army natives were beginning to get hostile, but I still pretended I was sleeping and didn't answer.

"Oh, my God! Johnson didn't say 'g'night,'" Lucas shouted. "Whatsa mattah with her?" She crawled out of bed and started shaking my arm. "Pal, are you okay? You always say 'g'night.' Pal?" I kept on pretending to be asleep and Lucas poked me harder.

"Johnson, are you okay? I can't see you breathing." I held my breath. "Oh, no! Johnson isn't breathing." Lucas started to panic. "She didn't say 'g'night.' She must be dead!" That really cracked me up, but Lucas didn't see me laughing because she was running out the door.

"Oh, my God!! Johnson's dead! Johnson's dead!" she screamed. A few seconds later, Sgt. Burke thundered down the hallway towards our room. As her heels clicked across the floor, I was suddenly sober. I realized my joke could get Lucas into serious trouble. If Sgt. Burke found out Lucas was drunk, she'd use it to try to make a case to kick her out of the Navy. I had to think fast.

"Johnson!" Sgt. Burke shook my arm.

"Yes, ma'am," I mumbled, rubbing my eyes and yawning.

"Are you all right?" For once, Sgt. Burke sounded like a human being. "Lucas thinks there's something wrong with you. She told me she thought you were dead."

"No, ma'am, I'm fine," I whispered so Lucas couldn't hear me. "She probably had a bad dream. Her twin sister was killed in an auto accident when she was very young and she sometimes has terrible nightmares. This has happened before. I'll take care of her. She'll be fine." I jumped down out of bed and went over to put my arm around Lucas. I gave Sgt. Burke a serious look.

"It would probably be better if you just left me alone with her," I said. Fortunately, she was still sleepy enough to take my advice.

"Okay, Johnson. But keep it quiet."

Lucas started babbling as soon as Sgt. Burke left the room. "Pal? Are you okay? I thought you were dead. You didn't say 'g'night.' "

"I'm fine," I said. "Let's just get you in bed now. Be quiet, okay? You woke everybody up."

"I'm sorry, pal," Lucas said. "I thought you were dead. I'm glad you're not." She was so upset that I started to feel guilty for tricking her.

"Okay." I patted her face. "Get some sleep."

In the morning, Lucas was furious when I told her the story.

"I never had a sister, you creep!" she said. "What a stupid story. Now everybody thinks I'm crazy. You ain't no pal of mine."

"Oh yes I am," I argued. "I could have told Sgt. Burke you were drunk. And you got me drunk, too. She knows I never drink. Then she would have made you go to alcohol rehab or kicked you out of the Navy. See what a pal I am?"

"Okay," Lucas grudgingly agreed. "But I still owe you one, Johnson."

5

Waves 1,
First Sergeant 0

"Ha! What did I tell you!" I gave Lucas a solid punch in the arm. The grades had been posted for the second month of school and I was one of the top three students. "You said I was wasting my time doing all that studying. You said I'd never be one of the top three students, but I did it. Now what do you have to say?" I smiled, imagining the look on Chief Hatch's face when he saw the grades.

"School ain't over yet," Lucas said as we walked from school to the barracks. "You still have to publish the winning newspaper and all you have is men on your staff."

I wasn't worried. The top three students were assigned as editors of a small newspaper as a final project. Students had to grade the other students on their own staff and those grades would be combined with the test scores to determine the honor graduates. The men on my staff were all good students and nice guys.

"You're such a party pooper, Lucas," I complained as we approached the barracks. As usual, there was a group of men sitting on the steps and draped over the railings in front. The men's Army barracks was right next door to ours, so there were always lots of men hanging around, looking at the women. Most of the fellas were pretty harmless; they were just annoying. But one young black Army private, James Washington, took great pleasure in scaring the girls, especially the white women. He was about six feet three inches tall, weighed at least two hundred pounds, and had obviously spent a great deal of his childhood making horrible faces in mirrors. Adults are always warning children that if they make mean, ugly faces too often, their faces will get stuck with mean, ugly expressions. Private Washington hadn't paid any attention to those warnings.

The first time I met Washington, I was standing in the doorway of the chow hall, waiting for Lucas to put her tray back.

"Hey, honky," a voice boomed from the sky above my head. "Move your ass. I'm tired of looking at your ugly motherfuckin' face."

A large belt buckle stood in front of my face. I tipped my head way back and looked up into Private Washington's face, a face that could not possibly have belonged to a person who possessed a sense of humor. I moved my ass out of his way real fast.

Naturally, when I noticed Private Washington sitting in the middle of the crowd of men on the barracks steps, I wasn't anxious for another little chat with him. I nudged Lucas. "There's Private Washington. Let's go around to the back entrance," I whispered.

Instead of turning, Lucas grabbed my arm and steered me toward the front steps. "Don't let him bother you, pal," she said. "He just thinks he's tough. He really isn't." Lucas was always bragging about a talent she supposedly possessed which allowed her to see right through people's attitudes into their real personalities. I didn't know what she saw, but I saw a very large, unfriendly person blocking the entrance of our barracks.

"Knock it off, Lucas." I tried to pull my arm free from her grip, but I had too many books in my hands. "Let's just go around to the back door," I said distinctly, through gritted teeth. Lucas held her ground.

"This is your chance to prove he isn't so tough," she said to me, then turned to the group of men and said, "Hey, Washington! My pal here has something she wants to say to you." My knees suddenly felt very weak. Lucas had lost her mind, right in front of my eyes.

"Is that right?" Washington stood up and stretched his arms over his head, yawning.

"N-no," I quickly stuttered, shaking my head so hard that I must have looked like one of those little spring-necked dogs that sit in the back window of strange and unusual people's cars. "My friend has you confused with someone else."

"Oh, I see," Washington said. "All us niggers look alike. Is that right?" Damn! I'd said the wrong thing, all right.

"No, that's not what I meant at all," I said, trying to smile, but only half my mouth cooperated. The other half just hung there, shaking. "Look, we'll just go around the back way. Don't bother moving. You just go on with your little meeting." But Washington had been challenged and he wasn't about to forget it so easily.

"I don't think so, honky bitch," he sneered. "If you got somethin' to say to me, why don't you say it? Or are you afraid your lily white skin will be contaminated from talkin' to a nigger?" I looked at Lucas, but she was no help. She was nudging a stone around in the dirt with the toe of her shoe.

"Race has nothing to do with this," I said. "My friend was only kidding, but she seems to have a rather warped sense of humor."

"You sayin' you'd have to be warped to talk to me, bitch?" This man was obviously unreceptive to excessive courtesy, so I decided to try a firmer attitude.

"Look," I said, this time managing to smile with my entire face. "My friend was only joking. I never did anything to you, so why don't you just leave us alone and quit blocking the steps?"

"That's right. You never did nothin' to me. But I got an idea of somethin' I can do to you, honky," he said, looking around as though to make sure the other men noticed his impressive display of poor grammar.

His words were tough, but something in his eyes told me that Lucas might be right about him. I decided to take a chance. I squared my shoulders, took a deep breath, and looked him straight in the eye.

"Private Washington," I said firmly. "I wholeheartedly support the U.S. Navy's policy on equal opportunity. And I truly believe that people should be judged by their character and not their color."

He didn't say anything, but he didn't kick me in the head, either, so I continued. "I'm getting tired of your picking on us because we're white women. We can't help being white any more than you can help being black. So why don't you just forget the tough guy act." I crossed my arms and stuck my chin in the air, trying to look real cocky. "If you're so tough, you can walk over here and beat me up. That'll show everyone how tough you really are."

Private Washington started walking slowly towards me. "Oh, shit, pal," Lucas gasped. "I didn't mean to get you killed." She backed up to a safe distance, leaving me to face Private Washington alone.

He walked up until he was so close that my nose almost touched his chest. Then he reached down and took my arm. His hand was so big that he could wrap his fingers all the way around my upper arm. I was too scared to move.

"Gentlemen, let's move aside and let these ladies walk up the steps," he said, to my amazement.

73

He looked down at me and wrinkled his lips. I think he tried to smile, but his smiler wasn't working any better than mine was that afternoon; mine was weak from fear, his had atrophied from lack of use.

"I like a woman with guts," he said as he slapped me lightly on the back, very nearly dislocating my shoulder.

Lucas returned to life as soon as we were safely inside the barracks.

"I told you I could tell if someone was really tough," she crowed as she ran around the room, jumping and clapping her hands. "Didn't I tell you, pal? Wasn't that exciting?" I could think of several more appealing ways to add excitement to my life. I could take a bus downtown at two o'clock in the morning and hang around in front of seedy hotels. Or I could wear a mini-skirt and hitchhike at midnight in front of a truck stop.

"Yeah, that was exciting, Lucas," I said, resisting the temptation to strangle her. "But stop jumping up and down for a minute because I have something to tell you." Lucas stopped in the middle of a jump, as she saw the menacing look in my eye.

"What's that, pal?" she asked.

"I owe you one, Lucas. A *big* one."

Standing double guard duty wasn't as bad as I expected it to be. At least I had Lucas to talk to, instead of some Army private who would make me wear my hat and follow all the regulations. For the first eight hours, we studied in between security checks of the building.

"Come on, pal," Lucas whined for the third time in ten minutes. "You aren't gonna get any smarter now. You think you're gonna prove something with your good grades? Ha! I betcha we both get orders to Norfolk. Every-

74

body in the Navy goes to Norfolk. Wanna bet? Come on, we'll play ninety-nine games of gin rummy and if I win the most games, I bet you get orders to Norfolk."

"That doesn't make any sense, Lucas," I said. "That's not a bet. But I'm just about studied out, so if you come up with a real bet, you're on."

She reconsidered and decided that we should bet a shoe-shine against a shirt ironing for our final personnel inspection at graduation. If I won, she would have to spit shine my shoes. If she won, I had to iron her shirt.

After six hours of cards, we were tied at forty-nine games apiece. Lucas took her turn touring the building to make sure it hadn't burned down while we weren't looking and I took the opportunity to stack the deck. Normally, I wouldn't have cheated my best pal, but I was desperate. I still hadn't learned to iron, and I didn't want to waste any time that I could spend in a last-minute cram session before the tests.

At eight o'clock the next morning, we packed up the cards and reported to class. We both managed to stay awake long enough to finish our exams. The lack of sleep must have helped me relax, because I got high scores. I was ecstatic until the grades from the newspaper staffs were posted. Every single man on my staff—Army, Navy, and Air Force alike—had given me a mediocre grade. I had spent hours agonizing over their grades, trying to be objective and fair. Despite my high test scores, my final class standing was fourth, just one notch below honor graduate.

"How could they do that to me, Lucas?" I asked. I was lying on my rack, looking at the ceiling, trying to understand the cruel world. Lucas sat on her rack, beneath mine, reading a magazine.

She tossed the magazine on the floor and flopped onto her stomach.

75

"I tried to tell you, pal," she said. "You spent all your time spitting on your shoes and doing your homework. I spent my time at the club, drinking sodas, playing cards, and swapping jokes with the guys. And we both got orders to Norfolk, where they really do have signs that say Dogs and Sailors Must Be on Leashes." She crawled off her bunk, stood up, and patted my arm. "I'm real sorry, pal, but maybe now you'll believe me when I tell you to relax," she said.

My grades had been so good that it never occurred to me that I might not get to choose my orders. It was all set in my mind. I'd go to the Philippine islands and eat mangoes in the sunshine and go swimming on Christmas Day. It was bad enough to lose out on my chance to go overseas, but the thing that really hurt my heart was that all the guys on my staff, who I thought were my friends, had stabbed me in the back.

"How could those guys do it to me, Lucas?" I asked, truly bewildered.

"Chief Hatch probably threatened them or something," she said. "But even if he didn't, they probably would have figured out a way to keep you from being an honor graduate. This is a man's Navy, pal, just like Chief Hatch says, and you're just gonna have to get that through your thick skull."

I still wasn't satisfied, but I had the orders in my hand. It said right there in black and white: Journalist Seaman Johnson assigned to report to the Public Affairs Office at Supreme Allied Command Atlantic, Norfolk, Virginia. At least Supreme Allied Command sounded exciting. And it was in the real Navy. The more I thought about going to Norfolk, the better it sounded. No more Army barracks. No more First Sergeant. There would be ships and sailors and adventures, for sure. I had visions of marching in and

76

saluting my new commanding officer. He'd shake my hand and welcome me aboard. Then I'd start making plans to visit all the exotic ports they advertise on the recruiting posters outside of the post office.

Lucas interrupted my daydreams. "Hey, pal There's one more thing I gotta do before we leave this place."

"Come on, Lucas, we're gonna miss our bus," I said as I checked my watch for the fifth time in four minutes. "We have to get to the airport on time. If we don't check into the Naval Station by midnight tonight, we'll be AWOL. It says right here on our orders. 'Check in by 0001.' That means one minute after midnight. See?" I shook my official orders in her face.

"I see, I see, but trust me. This will only take a minute. I *promise*," she pleaded.

I offered to wait by our luggage but she insisted that I had to go with her.

"It'll only take a minute," Lucas said, pulling on my arm. "We'll take a cab to the airport. I'll pay. But first I have to do something *very* important. I wouldn't lie to you. This is serious. Cross my heart and hope to spit." If Lucas was prepared to spit *and* pay for a cab, I knew it was hopeless to argue, so we left our luggage on the steps. I called a cab from the telephone booth outside the barracks and followed Lucas inside. She was unnaturally quiet as we walked over to First Sergeant Burke's office.

Lucas knocked softly on the door and silently winked at me as Sgt. Burke stood up and walked around her desk. She put her hands on her hips and sneered, "What do you two worms want? I'm sorry to see you go. I won't have anyone to volunteer for extra cleaning duty. What a pity."

Lucas looked down at the floor and shuffled her feet. I couldn't believe that my pal had made us miss our bus just so she could come over and give Sgt. Burke one last chance

77

to insult us. I turned to leave, but froze in my tracks when Lucas opened her mouth.

"I wanted to say good-bye, Sergeant Burke, and tell you that I don't have any hard feelings towards you even though you took every opportunity to give me a bad time. You made me stand extra watches and do extra cleaning duty, even when I didn't do anything wrong. But I know you must have had a good reason."

I stood in the hallway, dumbfounded, staring at my friend.

"That's right, Lucas," Sgt. Burke said, rubbing her hands together. "I gave you extra duty because you're a punk." She looked at me. "You're both punks, coming here and taking all your fancy writing courses. I never took any courses. I never even finished high school and look where I am today."

"Yes, ma'am," Lucas agreed. "You really have come a long way, in charge of a whole barracks." Lucas had clearly lost her mind.

"That's right," said the sergeant. "I give the orders around here and I showed you, didn't I? You think you're so smart, but I knocked you down a peg or two. And, by the way, I enjoyed it." What a creep. I figured by now that Lucas would have come to her senses and would stop sniveling so we could leave. But I knew Lucas had really gone over the edge when she extended her right hand to Sgt. Burke. My pal was going to shake hands with the most disgusting woman I'd ever met!

Sgt. Burke put her hand out and Lucas firmly grasped it. Then she quickly reached down and lifted the sergeant up, carried her out into the hallway, and dropped her into a large trash barrel.

"Come on, Johnson!" she yelled, as she dashed out the door. "Don't just stand there. We gotta catch that cab or we'll be real sorry."

I took off after Lucas, running down the hallway at top speed, looking back over my shoulder to see if Sgt. Burke was after us. All I could see were the tops of her shiny black shoes, kicking a fountain of papers out of the barrel. We had plenty of time to get off the base and on our way to the airport.

Lucas stopped suddenly.

"Attention!" she hollered. "I have written a little song in honor of the occasion." We saluted Sgt. Burke as Lucas sang:

From the shores of San Diego
To the barracks of Fort Ben,
We will fight our best to overcome
Army creeps and macho men.
We'll ignore the extra duties
And the nasty cracks about "gals."
But we'll always have the final laugh
'Cause we're the famous Navy Pals!

"Lucas, you certainly have a way with words. Ever thought of being a writer?" I grabbed the luggage we had left in front of the barracks. Our cab was waiting outside —just like a movie getaway.

"It sounds like a nice job, pal," Lucas said, "but I'm not trained for it. I went to journalism school, but I spent most of my time peeing in bottles. Think I could get a job doing that?"

"I think if anybody could, you could."

Lucas removed her hat, bowed, and ushered me into the cab with a flourish.

"You got faith in me, Johnson," she said as we sped away from the barracks. "What a pal!"

6

This Man's Navy

At boot camp, I knew the male recruits weren't studying Etiquette and learning how to sit like perfect gentlemen, but I never had a chance to ask them what subjects were included in their curriculum, since intermingling of the sexes was strictly forbidden and severely punished. The only time we were authorized to talk to the men was in church. When the CC announced that seating was coed during religious services, our entire company found the Lord. Of course, once we got close enough to flirt with the men, we were too busy trying to wriggle our hips like shameless hussies to think about our academic training.

When I got to Norfolk, it took me about four minutes to figure out that while the women were learning to be dainty Waves, the male recruits were being molded into macho swabbies. After seeing them in action, it was obvious that they received intense training in all the important "s" subjects:

Spitting
Swearing
Swaggering
Sniffing (while hitching up pants by the belt buckle)
Selecting tattooes (nude women, huge breasts, dragons, eagles, etc.)

Smoking cigarettes à la Humphrey Bogart
Screaming vulgar comments at females

On my first day in the Fleet, several macho course hon-
or graduates lounged against the railing, watching me
drag my luggage up the steps of the women's barracks.
None of them offered to help me carry my bags, but one
of them informed me that I was welcome to eat crackers
in his bed and another asked me if I liked to eat hot
dogs.

In the lobby of the barracks was a lounge with dilapi-
dated green vinyl sofas, a color TV that was bolted to the
floor, and a soft drink machine with a THIS DON'T WORK
sign taped to its front. I dragged my suitcases through the
lounge and joined the line of people in front of a desk
bearing a plaque that read Master-at-Arms. On the wall to
the left of the desk was a large handwritten sign:

Barracks Rules and Regulations

1. No spitting on the decks or ladders.
2. Members of the oppasit sex may visit rooms from
    1000 to 2200 daily. During visits, the door must
    stay open and at least one foot of each person
    must be placed firmly on the floor.
3. Dirty linen must be exchanged for clean linen by
    0900 Thursdays. If you don't have your filthy
    sheets in the hallway by then, sleep on them for
    another week, you slime bags.
4. Brake the chairs in the lounge and you buy them.
5. Rooms are inspected each Friday at 0800. If you
    want to live in a pig sty, move to a farm.
              PO1 Clyde Hawkins, Master-at-Arms

On a table in front of the desk was another sign: "If you
ain't been hear before, sign these."

81

I could hardly wait to meet Petty Officer Hawkins. He was obviously a charming fella as well as a champion speller. A tall girl with curly red hair stood at the head of the line in front of the check-in desk. She had three stripes and an eagle on her left sleeve and, from the way she ignored the comments of the men hanging around the lobby, I guessed that she'd been in the Navy for a while. PO Hawkins handed her a stack of envelopes and she walked away from the desk, sorting through her mail. As she passed the crowd of guys, one of them reached out and grabbed her butt. Without looking up, she brushed his hand off as though it were a pesky fly.

"Your mother is a sow, Felton," she said over her shoulder as she nonchalantly walked up the stairs. I hoped I would get a room near hers, even though I knew we wouldn't be roommates. Only people of the same rank were assigned to share rooms, but I wanted to ask her how she learned to handle men so well. I was busy gawking around and didn't notice that it was my turn to check in.

Hawkins snatched the check-in sheets from my hand and glared at me through the cigarette smoke that drifted upwards from the bent cigarette that clung to his lower lip. He had four raggedy ribbons tacked over his pocket, three stripes and an eagle on his left shirt sleeve, two tattoos on each forearm, and a belly that hung over his belt.

He glanced at my orders, then snorted and hollered, "Lookee here, fellas, we got us a virgin sailor girl checkin' in. This is her first duty station. Which one of you wants to volunteer to be her new roommate so's you can break her in right?"

He didn't wait for an answer before he turned back to me and said, "Don't bother actin' indignant, honey. I know you wouldn't of joined the Navy if you was really a lady.

Ladies stay at home with their husbands or their mamas. The girls with hot pants join the Navy so's they can get some of that good U.S. Department of the Navy grade-A meat. I run a tight ship here, so don't let me catch you screwin' around in my barracks."

I was too shocked to say anything, so I just stood there and stared at him as he sniffed, hitched up his pants, and belched.

"This is a man's Navy, sweetheart, and women only have three positions where they really belong—on their backs, on their bellies, and on their way out the door."

This wasn't the Navy I had expected. I'd planned to march in, salute sharply, and be welcomed aboard by my commanding officer. Then I'd begin writing wonderful press releases and making plans to travel to exotic ports. My chin started to quiver and I fought to keep from crying.

"Hawkins, you asshole! Why do you have to harass all the new women?" The girl I had seen earlier had come to my rescue. Nearly six feet tall, she stood looking down at Hawkins, with her hands on her hips, her eyes blazing. The fire-colored hair tumbling wildly around her shoulders only made her seem more fierce.

"You're the sorriest excuse for a petty officer that I've ever seen," she snapped. "If your brother-in-law wasn't an admiral, you'd be out of here in a flash. And you have a lot of nerve talking about women lying on their bellies." She poked her finger into the soft flesh that swelled above Hawkins's belt. "You're just jealous because you couldn't lie on your fat belly to save your soul, you slob."

Hawkins glared at her for a minute, obviously trying to think of a retort. Then, noticing her hair, he said, "You ain't allowed to wear your hair down in uniform, Miss Smarty Pants Petty Officer."

"For your information," she said, "I was combing my

hair when I heard you down here making an ass of yourself again, Hawkins." She grabbed my check-in sheet out
of Hawkins's hand and turned to me. "Come on, honey. I
can tell you're gonna need some help getting used to this
place. My name's Ski. Actually, it's Ursula Marie Du-
brokowski, but you can see why no one calls me that. Most
of us call each other by our last names, just like in basic
training. There seems to be a Navy regulation against
having first names. What's your name?"

She started talking again before I could answer.

"Where are you from?" she asked, then held up her
hand. "Wait. Let me guess." She looked me over quickly.
"The Midwest. I'm right, aren't I?"

"Close," I said, surprised. "I'm from Youngsville, Pennsylvania—'Biggest Little Town on the Map.' But how did
you know where I was from?"

Ski leaned forward. "Don't take this as an insult, but
you got 'hick' written all over you," she said, as she tapped
a finger on my chest. Then, she turned her hand and tapped
her own chest. "I'm from New York City myself, so I was
used to living with the wild animals. This Navy life is a trip,
but don't let those jerks discourage you. They aren't all
like that. Lots of the guys around here are real gentlemen."

Ski didn't stop talking the entire time that she showed
me around the barracks, demonstrating how to kick the air
conditioner to make it work, advising me to double lock my
locker so no one could steal my valuables when I was out
of my cube. No rooms, just corrugated plastic cubicles like
the ones in boot camp. The cubicles weren't very large and
they weren't very private, but they also weren't painted
Army olive drab. Better yet, they weren't down the hall
from a First Sergeant's office. PO Hawkins wasn't much
of an improvement over Sgt. Burke, but at least he had to

leave our barracks at night and sleep in a different building.

Brightly colored shower curtains hung in place of doors, which softened the look of the plastic cubicles. Most of the walls were covered with travel posters, but the walls didn't go all the way to the floor and if I stood on tiptoe, I could see over the top of them. I was thrilled to see that there were only two women per cube. I checked out the head at the end of the hall and was delighted to see that the showers had partitions. No more group hygiene! A step in the right direction, at least. With each new assignment, I was moving closer to that badge of success—a private room with a bath. It wasn't just professional pride or patriotism that motivated the Waves to excel in their chosen fields. It was also the knowledge that with rank comes the privilege of sleeping, dressing, and bathing in privacy! Civilians just breeze in and out of their private bathrooms without giving the matter much thought, but toilets are serious business to Waves and a private toilet is something to be earned and greatly appreciated.

"You'd be surprised what I've seen in my five years in this Navy, honey," Ski continued as I inspected my new home. "But we got a nice bunch of girls living here, so you'll have fun. Most of the guys are okay, too, if you talk to them alone, but don't ever try to talk to them when they're in a group. They turn into animals."

"So I noticed," I said, remembering my recent encounter with Hawkins and his cohorts.

Ski finally paused for breath and left me to unpack. We arranged to meet in a little while to walk to the enlisted men's club for a steak dinner. Waves were allowed to go to the club, but it was still called the enlisted men's club because that's what it had always been called. I was putting my clothes in my locker when the shower curtain on my doorway blew open.

"I shoulda known you'd be folding your underwear in little squares, you lifer!" Lucas breezed in, tossed her duffle bag on the floor, rushed over with outstretched arms, and punched me in both shoulders at once.

"Lucas!" When I saw her familiar grin, I realized just how lonely I had been feeling. "I can't believe it! Are you my cubemate?"

"Lucky for you there aren't any females in this barracks whose last names begin with K," she informed me, "because otherwise you wouldn't have the pleasure of sharing living quarters with me. The women's barracks at the base where I work isn't finished yet. I have to ride a bus to work in the mornings until the construction is done."

"Me, too."

"Of course, the admiral—we're old pals—offered to let me use his car to drive to work," Lucas continued, "but I forgot to bring my personal flag to hang on the front. So I guess I'll just ride the bus."

"I have to ride a bus to work, too. We must work on the same base!" I said. "I'm assigned to the Public Affairs Office at the Supreme Allied Command Atlantic—they call it SACLANT. But that's not where you got assigned, is it?"

"No, I'm at the Public Affairs Office for the Commander-in-Chief Atlantic Fleet—CINCLANT. They're on the same base, though." Lucas grinned and punched me on the arm again. "I guess we're neighbors."

"Quit punching me and get your stuff put away," I said. "I met this real neat first-class petty officer and she's gonna take me to dinner at the EM club. You can come with us. Boy, it's great to see you, pal!"

"How come you're so happy to see me?" Lucas asked. "You always say I'm a pain in the ass."

"I know, but I haven't forgotten that I owe you a big one. Remember Private Washington?" I certainly did.

"Unfortunately, I do," Lucas admitted. "But you have to admit that was pretty neat, Johnson." She poked me in the ribs and tried to charm me with her biggest smile.

"Yeah, that was neat," I said. "But you're a slob. You're gonna have to shape up if you want to live in my cube."

"I always knew you were a lifer, Johnson," Lucas said, as Ski walked in.

"Who's a lifer?" she asked. Lucas took one look at the stripes on Ski's arm and the ribbons on her shirt and started coughing.

"I didn't say *lifer*," she told Ski. "I said, 'You're the best pal I ever had in my *life*, Johnson. That's what I said." She stuck out her hand, "Glad to meet you."

Ski shook hands with Lucas and immediately began dispensing more advice, as she showed us the quickest route to walk to the enlisted men's club. En route, we approached a bus stop where a gang of sailors were gathered.

"Oh-oh," Ski whispered. "Just keep your mouths shut and let me handle this."

"Mmm. I sure would like to eat that candy!"

"Yeah. Look at those delectable drumsticks."

"How'd you like some nice hot cum in your snatch, baby?"

I froze in mid-step. I felt dirty, as though the sailor had spit right in my face. Even Lucas, who liked to claim that nothing could shock her, gasped and blushed. But Ski didn't even flinch. She kept right on walking until she stood face to face with the sailor who had spoken loudest and last.

"Excuse me, but I didn't hear what you gentlemen were saying," she said in a dignified, feminine voice. "If you do have something to say, I certainly hope you are men enough to say it to my face."

That particular man didn't have anything to say, but as we walked away, another one mumbled, "Boy, that twat thinks she's hot shit, doesn't she?"

Ski did a quick about-face. This time she spoke in her regular New York voice. "Is that the way your mother taught you to talk to women, sailor? If so, she would be mighty proud of her son if she could hear you now, wouldn't she?" She waited for his answer, but he didn't respond.

Ski continued her indoctrination course as we walked on. In most cases it was best to ignore the rowdy sailors, she said. But, if you had to get tough, it was best to confront each macho male as an individual person.

"It's a heck of a lot easier for these guys to treat you bad if they don't know you," Ski explained. "It's kind of like hating cops because all they ever do is harass people. But when a cop moves next door to you with his family and you see that he's a regular person who has to take out a second mortgage to pay his utility bills, the same as you do, he isn't such a creep." I nodded.

"It's the same way with these fellas," Ski said. "It's a pain in the neck, but if you take the time to talk to them, they think of you as a person and treat you a heck of a lot better. Most of them are just lonely and want some attention. But they don't know how to ask for it politely."

"Don't you ever get tired of being so tough all the time?" I asked. I couldn't picture myself not getting upset when men talked to me like that.

"Sure," Ski admitted. "Sometimes I just let them think they got the best of me. If they get too nasty, I mention their mothers. That seems to get their attention."

I motioned toward Ski's rating badge. "Why don't you

just put them on report?" I said. "You outrank most of the sailors on this base."

Ski shook her head. "That's a last resort. It isn't worth the hassle," she said. "If you write them up, they know they got to you." She tapped a finger against her temple. "If they think they can make you mad or, better yet, make you cry, they'll harass you forever." She smiled mysteriously and raised her eyebrows. "Sometimes it even pays to let a guy be macho. If you cut a man enough slack, he'll usually hang himself with it."

I tried to digest all this new information along with my dinner at the club. It was a gigantic place with two large dance floors surrounded by several tiers of tables. Before the dancing began, there was a short-order grill in operation on the top tier. We took our dinner trays to one of the tables and were enjoying our meal in the nearly empty club. Most of the enlisted people ate in the chow hall because we were issued passes to eat there for free.

I was busy gawking at the purple velvet wallpaper and the chandeliers, so I didn't pay much attention to the two sailors who sat down at the table next to ours. There must have been a hundred empty tables in the room, but they chose to sit near us.

"Would either of you ladies care to dansh?" One of the sailors was swaying beside our table.

"Thank you very much," Ski said, "but we're eating our dinner right now." She smiled politely at the sailor and returned her attention to her dinner.

"I asked you if you wanna dansh, ya stupid bitch!" the sailor yelled, obviously drunk.

"I told you we are eating our dinner at this moment and there isn't any dance music right now, anyway," Ski said, still polite, but a little less friendly.

Lucas was keeping her mouth shut, which had me worried. The only time she ever got quiet was when she was up to something devious.

"What'd you stupid bitches come here for if you don't wanna dansh?" the sailor said. Ski started to get out of her chair. She had told us that her boyfriend taught her how to lift weights and she was proud of her strength. I hoped she wouldn't get in a fist fight because I knew I'd be like one of those stupid women in the movies who just stand there and watch their friends get killed.

Before Ski could stand up, Lucas jumped to her feet. She reached over and took a cigarette out of the pack in the sailor's shirt pocket, lit it with a match from the ashtray on the table, and started puffing wildly. She stood quietly in her cloud of smoke for a few seconds, face to face with the surprised sailor. Then she blew a mouthful of smoke in his face, patted him on the head, and said, "Son, we're trying to eat our dinner. So I suggest you sit your drunk little butt down over there in your own chair and mind your manners."

Then she gave him what she called her "eat shit and die" look. It worked. He didn't know how to respond to her bizarre antics. He stood there for a minute with his mouth hanging open and a little trickle of saliva running down his chin. Then he swayed back and forth, turned around, and staggered back to sit with his buddy.

Lucas asked Ski to show her where the restroom was, leaving me to to stand guard over our dinner. As soon as they were out of sight, the other sailor came over and sat down in Ski's chair. He looked at my breasts and my crotch, slid his chair closer, and put his arm around my shoulder, holding me tightly so I couldn't stand up.

"You sure are a good-lookin' piece, you know," he said.

I tried to move his arm, but he didn't loosen his grip.

"Why do you girls keep playin' hard to get?" he asked.

"We know what you women join the Navy for. You like men. That's nothin' to be ashamed of."

He reached up and grabbed a handful of my hair. I couldn't decide whether to scream or try to punch him in the face. His breath smelled terrible, but he didn't seem to be as drunk as his friend.

Suddenly a hand gripped his elbow and he dropped my hair in surprise.

Ski had returned from the restroom with Lucas right behind her, and I could tell from the looks on their faces that they were up to something. Ski squinted her eyes real small.

"Would you mind removing yourself from my chair, sailor?" she said. "I'd like to finish my dinner."

He didn't move. A few other sailors had wandered into the club and were drawn to our table by the loud voices. No one, including the bouncer, made an effort to help us, so Ski forged ahead.

"I asked you nicely to remove yourself from my chair, sailor," she said.

"If you want me to move, why don't you move me?" He gave her a belligerent look.

"Are you sure that's what you want me to do, sailor?" Ski asked sweetly. With all those men watching him, he couldn't back down. He had to be cool.

"Who are you kiddin'? You ain't big enough to move me," he said.

"Put your money where your mouth is, sailor," Ski answered. "Twenty bucks says I can move you out of that chair."

He had no choice but to put his twenty dollars on the table. Lucas turned to the spectators. "Any of you fellas want to lose twenty?" she asked. A handful of twenties slapped down on the table.

Ski took a deep breath, put one arm around the sailor's back, and put the other behind his knees. She grunted loudly, lifted him a few inches off the chair, then coughed and dropped him.

"Just a minute," she gasped. "I can't get my breath. My belt's too tight." She winked at me as she adjusted her belt. More twenties hit the table.

"Okay." She leaned over and picked up the sailor in one swift motion. No one made a sound as she carried him to his table, dropped him into his chair, blew a kiss to the stunned onlookers, and stuffed the bills into her pocket. Ski was right—sometimes it pays to let men be macho! We made three hundred dollars.

"Come on," I whispered. "Let's get out of here." I wanted to leave before any more sailors had a chance to stop by our table for some scintillating conversation. "My mother always said it was a good idea to leave a party while you're still having fun. That way you have only fond memories."

"Your mother sounds like a real smart lady, Johnson," Lucas said, as she stood up and pushed her chair under the table. "How come you're so dumb?" Ski thought Lucas was real amusing, so the two of them stood laughing like a couple of idiots.

"Go ahead, Lucas, add them up," I threatened. "I already owe you one. You two hyenas just stand there and laugh for a while. I'm going to the head." I huffed.

Just as I reached the restroom, a boyish-looking sailor approached me.

"Excuse me, miss," he said politely. He had that all-American, freshly scrubbed look. With his shaved head, he looked like he was about eight years old. I expected him to ask me what time it was or if I wanted to dance now that the band had started.

92

"Will you fuck me?" he asked in the same soft voice.

"I beg your pardon?" I coughed, sure that he had not said what I thought I heard.

"Will you fuck me?" he repeated.

It was like a bad dream that kept going on after I woke up. First Hawkins, then the drunk sailors, and now this baby-faced kid. Suddenly I was overwhelmed with the fact that maybe I wasn't quite prepared to face life in the real Navy. Apparently, the kid realized I was in a state of semi-shock.

"My ship's going out to sea for six months tomorrow," he said. "I don't have a girl to write to or anything and the girls in town hate sailors and I'm so lonely. I just want to be with a real girl, not a hooker." He looked like he was going to start crying any minute, so I decided not to punch him in the nose.

Instead, I walked into the restroom. I looked in the mirror and saw a familiar reflection. Brown eyes, wavy brown hair, turned-up nose, slight overbite. But the drawn, white face belonged to a stranger.

"What in the world am I doing here?" I asked the girl in the mirror, as she asked me the same question. Neither one of us answered.

Lucas and Ski thought the young sailor's proposition was absolutely hilarious.

"You gotta admit," Lucas laughed, "the kid definitely had a unique approach." When she realized that I was actually shocked and embarrassed, she grew serious.

"Aw, come on, pal. He was probably just pulling your leg," she said. "You look so dumb and innocent, these guys get a kick out of making you blush."

"Don't worry about it, Johnson." Ski put her arm around my shoulder. "I told you there were a lot of nice guys around here. You just happened to meet a whole group of rejects your very first day on board. We'll go back to the barracks and get a good night's sleep and everything will look brighter in the morning."

The barracks had been dim and deserted when we left for dinner, since everyone was still at work. Now the lights were blazing and women sat in the lounge and on the floors in between the cubicles, talking and laughing. A big crowd was gathered around the mirror in the head, putting on makeup, curling their hair, and dressing in preparation for their dates that evening.

A blond woman, barely five feet tall, approached us as we entered the barracks. "Nice try, Ski, but you didn't miss Field Night," she said with a smile. "We managed to do most of the cleaning without you, but we saved the lounge for you so you wouldn't feel left out. We swabbed it, but it needs to be waxed and buffed."

"Johnson, Lucas"—Ski pointed at us—"I'd like you to meet Big Bertha. She's the senior enlisted woman in the barracks, so she's in charge of all the fun things like making sure we have Field Night, no male visitors after hours, no booze in our rooms. She's the resident party pooper."

Bertha laughed and shook her head. "Give me a break, Ski. If it weren't for me, Hawkins would have your ass for mouthing off to him all the time. I spend most of my time keeping you girls out of trouble."

Bertha shook hands with me and Lucas, then turned and yelled, "Now hear this! We got two new girls here, ladies —Johnson and Lucas. Treat them right and help them out if you see them in trouble." Greetings came from all directions.

"Welcome aboard!"

"If either of you plays tennis, stop by Cube 3!"

94

"Don't go out with Mark McKinney—he's a pig!"

"Tuesday nights are gin rummy nights in the lounge!"

Meanwhile, Ski had gone to get two swabs from the gear locker down the hall. She handed one to each of us. "You two wax the floor of this luxurious dwelling and I'll handle the buffer."

I was amazed. "You mean you can use a buffer all by yourself?" I asked.

Ski pulled up her sleeve and tensed her biceps. "I'm pretty strong, remember?" Her posing session was interrupted by shrieks and curses, as a husky young Marine ran into the hallway, followed by three women armed with brooms and mops.

"You pervert!" screamed one girl, as she swung the broom, smacking the guy across his shins and knocking him to the floor. Another girl rushed up and began beating him with a wet mop. Three more girls joined in, and the poor guy started screaming for mercy. Bertha managed to pull the women off him. "Okay, what's the story here?" she demanded.

"This pervert crawled in one of the windows," explained the girl with the mop. "He was trying to steal all my panties. He said he made a bet with his buddies that Waves were so eager, he could get the pants off six of us in one night. What a creep!" She smacked the Marine with her mop.

Bertha had to guard the captured pantie snitcher until the military police arrived on the scene, blowing their whistles and brandishing their nightsticks. They arrested the Marine, but didn't take him directly to the brig. Instead, they took him to the dispensary. Those women really knew how to handle their cleaning gear. They had broken his collarbone and cracked one of his ribs!

"What do you think, Lucas?" I asked after the excitement died down and we finally hit our racks. "Did we make a mistake joining the Navy?"

"Naw, pal," came her confident voice, from across the room. "We just gotta get used to being in the Fleet. Pretty soon we'll be salty sailors and we'll go around swapping sea stories. We'll have a good one to tell about today, won't we?"

"We sure will," I agreed. "But I hope the men we work with aren't like the turkeys we met today."

"They couldn't possibly all be like that," Lucas said. She paused. "Could they?"

7

R.H.I.P.—Rank Has Its Privileges

There were fifteen people assigned to the staff of the Public Affairs Office of the Supreme Allied Commander Atlantic—fourteen men and me. Finally, I had my chance to salute a real live commanding officer, Captain Snelling. After I saluted, he shook my hand and gave me a brisk talk on doing my best to be a top-notch journalist and squared-away Navy woman. He explained that I would be writing press releases, preparing speeches, and fulfilling other duties as assigned in support of Admiral Packard P. Danworthy, the Supreme Allied Commander Atlantic.

"Other duties" turned out to be my main occupation. I made coffee, emptied trash cans, filed paperwork, swept the floor, and picked up the office supplies. Since I was the lowest-ranking enlisted person, I got all the "little bitty shitty" jobs as my supervisor, Chief Bagget, liked to call them. It took a while, but I finally understood why the sailors in the office had given me such a warm welcome. They all outranked me.

"You gotta do your time, just like any other sailor," Chief Bagget said when I complained. He was a big man, over six feet tall, with dark brown hair. Actually, he had a dark brown beard. The rest of his head was completely bald.

"When the next person checks in," the chief assured me,

"you won't be junior and then you can do some real writing. But right now, you pay your dues."

"When do you think the next person will check in, Chief?" I asked.

"Oh, probably a year or so," he replied.

"I can hardly wait."

Chief Bagget took a sip from the coffee cup on his desk. His coffee cup, his paperweight, his letter opener—everything in his office that could be stamped or engraved—bore the same gold anchor insignia that gleamed on the collar of his shirt.

"You won't get any sympathy from the sailors around here, Johnson," the chief said, nodding his head toward the group. "This is the first time that most of these guys have ever worked with a woman. They've been out on ships, where life isn't so easy. Sometimes they only get to take one shower a week because the water rations are running low. And they sleep in smelly little cubby holes, stand duty every other day, and work their butts off."

He went on, describing life at sea in great detail—the long hours standing watch on the deck in the howling wind and rain, sleepless nights as the ship was tossed by huge waves, months without a letter from home or a hug from a woman. As he spoke, I felt ashamed for complaining because I didn't have a private shower at the barracks. Because of me, some poor, unwashed, and homesick sailor was being tossed to and fro in his hard little rack at night. By the time the chief stopped talking, I felt guilty that I even had a building to sleep inside.

"These guys finally get to shore duty," the chief concluded, "and they find a lot of their old jobs filled by Waves. Seems to them that every woman in a shore billet is taking away a chance for them to stay on dry land for a while. So some of them aren't particularly fond of female sailors. You understand?"

"But, Chief," I argued, "women have been in the Navy for thirty years. What's the big deal?"

"Waves used to be restricted to admin jobs, or nursing," he said. "Now they're aircraft mechanics and boatswain's mates." He shook his head. "Don't you understand why that bothers some of the men? They think their Navy is being invaded."

"Women have just as much right to serve their country as men do," I told the chief. I politely reminded him that no one forces men to join the Navy; enlistment is entirely voluntary. And, furthermore, it wasn't the women's fault that they couldn't work onboard ships. U.S. law and Navy regulations prohibited women from seagoing billets—partially because of the possibility of combat, partially because it simply hadn't been done before.

"You better thank your lucky stars you aren't out on a ship with a bunch of sailors, woman," he said. He had a good point. Considering how they acted on land, I could just imagine how much fun it would be if I were a captive audience at sea.

"I never thought of that before, Chief."

"That's why I'm a chief," he said. "I think real good. Now, I think you better get this filing done and get out of here before the XO gets done with his meeting. He said he wanted to talk to you, but I can forget to tell you just this once."

Chief Bagget did his best to protect me from the XO—Commander Wendell Rodney Wadsworth III, my executive officer. The XO was pompous, overbearing, crude, anti-feminist, and with a vile sense of humor. He took great delight in making derogatory remarks about my moral character, mental ability, and reason for joining the service. He frequently remarked that Navy women were either husband hunters or whores. Then he would leer at me and ask me which one I was.

At first, I naively thought that Commander Wadsworth didn't realize how upsetting his remarks were. I told him that he embarrassed me and he replied that I was too sensitive. He added that, since he was my boss, I had better learn to laugh at his jokes or he would consider my behavior disrespectful. I did my best to avoid him when possible and ignored him when necessary.

One morning, after I had been onboard for about three months, Commander Wadsworth sent one of the sailors to the cafeteria to buy some doughnuts to serve at an impromptu office staff meeting. When the sailor had been gone longer than expected, the XO swaggered over to my desk and said, "We didn't have to send Dwayne all the way to Hawaii to get a pig for our little luau. We have a pig right here." He pointed at me and leered as all the men in the office roared with laughter.

I was furious. Back home, my brothers would have beat the stuffing out a man who called their sister a pig, but I didn't have any brothers to protect me in the Navy and the man outranked me by a mile, so I politely asked Commander Wadsworth to stop making such insulting remarks. I thought if I asked him in front of the guys, he'd be embarrassed. It didn't work. Instead, he just pounded my desk with his fist and told me not to be disrespectful.

Later that day, I yawned while shuffling some papers as the XO happened to be passing through the office. "If you enlisted women didn't spend all your nights having lesbian orgies in the barracks, you wouldn't be so tired at work," he jeered.

I bit my lip and managed to keep my mouth shut, but he just wouldn't quit. Later that morning, officers from fifteen different NATO countries gathered in front of our building for a flag-raising ceremony. I happened to be standing near a captain in the Royal Netherlands Navy, Captain Lindstrom. The night before, I had been assigned to the fire watch while Captain Lindstrom was the duty officer. The captain slept in a bunkroom in another building on base, where he would be available in case of an emergency, while I stood guard at the desk in the front of the building.

As the ceremony ended, the XO strolled over and stood beside me. "I hear you had the watch last night with Captain Lindstrom," he said loudly.

"Yessir," I answered.

"I hear that you enjoyed *doing your duty* last night. But you did complain that the sheets were already dirty!" he said. The foreign officers standing nearby frowned and looked at me, not quite sure they understood what the XO had said. Others snickered and looked at me as though they understood exactly what he meant and believed him. Humiliated and angry, I rushed into the office, swept the papers off my desk, and grabbed my purse. Chief Bagget rushed in and tried to talk to me, but I pushed him aside and stomped out of the building, yelling, "I'm sick of being talked to like a whore just because I'm an enlisted woman! If Commander Wadsworth ever talks to me again, I'm gonna kick him in the balls. Tell him to stuff that in his officer's hat!"

On the ride to the barracks, I sat in the back of the bus and sobbed. Once inside my cube, I threw myself down on the bed and cried myself to sleep. Lucas woke me up when she came home from work and I told her the story, which set me off crying again.

"Now I'm in big trouble because I ran away from work," I blubbered.

"Geez, pal," Lucas agreed. "You *are* in big trouble. You were disrespectful to your XO *and* you're AWOL. You could get court-martialed, I bet!" That really made me howl.

When I finally calmed down, we spent the evening trying to come up with a plan to get me out of trouble, but we couldn't change the facts. I was in big trouble, so I decided to take my punishment with dignity. The next morning, I walked quietly into the office and sat down at my desk. All the men stopped talking and looked at me, anxious for the excitement to begin.

They didn't have to wait long. In a few minutes, Commander Wadsworth walked over to my desk and asked me if I was still speaking to him. I didn't think I could get in any more trouble at that point, so I just shut my eyes and wished he would go away. I got my wish, but he left behind a dozen red roses. As he left the room, he turned and said, "I'm sorry. I'll never talk to you that way again."

The men were furious.

"Jesus H. Christ! A crying dame will get them every time!"

"Shit, if she was a man, he'd bust her ass for sure!"

"Waves get all the breaks in this Navy. What a pisser!"

They insisted that the XO didn't bust me for disrespect to a senior officer and leaving my duty post without permission just because I was a female.

Chief Bagget interrupted their complaints by calling me into his office for a private talk. I was prepared for a long lecture on my disgusting behavior. When he shut the door to ensure privacy, I knew I was in trouble.

"Johnson," the chief began, "you learned a valuable lesson today, didn't you?"

"Yes, I did, Chief," I agreed.

"When a senior officer steps out of line to harass you, he steps on his own tail," the chief continued. "If he tries to bust you for defending yourself, he'll have to explain to the Old Man, Admiral Danworthy, what he did to you in the first place." I was flabbergasted. The idea that an officer could get in trouble for picking on me had never entered my mind.

"You mean Commander Wadsworth could get in trouble for harassing me all the time just because I'm a female?" I asked.

"That's right," the chief nodded. "It's against Navy policy to harrass people because of their sex, race, or religion. Now that you understand, Johnson, remember it. But don't abuse that knowledge."

Lucas was delighted by the story and the flowers.

"Excellent work, pal." She sniffed a rose, then tucked it into her lapel and admired herself in front of the mirror. "This adds a nice touch, don't you think?" she asked. "Next time I see the admiral, I think I'll suggest making roses a mandatory uniform requirement on Mondays." She sat down on her bunk and grinned at me. "I wish I could have been these to see the commander give you those roses."

"Yeah, you missed a great sea story," I said as I quickly hung up my uniform and changed into my civilian clothes.

"Hey! I have an idea, Lucas," I said. "Why don't you buy me a beer to celebrate that I didn't get busted? You just cashed your paycheck, didn't you?"

Lucas looked at me in surprise. She usually had to twist my arm to get me to drink a beer. "All right!" she agreed. "Now you're starting to talk like a sailor. Let's go!"

Lucas was still wearing her uniform when we walked into the small club. I noted with delight that she was too involved in listening to a story of mine to remember to take off her hat. We each took a bar stool and I coughed loudly several times to make sure everyone in the club noticed us. Within seconds, a bell began ringing and all the people in the club cheered.

"Thank you, little lady!"

"Make mine a double."

"All right! I always said it was nice to have Waves around!"

"What's going on here, pal?" Lucas asked.

I put my arm around her shoulder. "I'm so sorry, Lucas. If I had noticed that you were still wearing your hat, I *certainly* would have told you to take it off."

Lucas gave me a blank look.

"Don't tell me you forgot that old Navy tradition." I slapped myself on the forehead. "If you wear your hat into the club and someone rings the bell before you take off your hat, you have to buy everyone in the club a round of drinks."

"Shit!" Lucas pulled off her hat and threw it down on the bar.

"Your memory is getting pretty bad," I said. "I'll bet you forgot that I owe you one for Private Washington, too." I kept my arm around her shoulder so she couldn't jump off her bar stool and knock me down. "Isn't it lucky that you just cashed your paycheck?" I asked. "Lucky, too, that there are only about ten people in here."

Lucas grabbed my collar with her free hand and pulled my face close to hers. "You could die for this, Johnson," she hissed. She tried to look fierce, but I could tell she was impressed. Even Lucas had to admit that I gave her a good "gotcha."

I shrugged and blinked my wide, innocent eyes at her. "Don't blame me, pal. I had nothing to do with it. It's just an old Navy tradition."

8

Susie Civilian

"Oh no! Tell me it isn't true! Look at this!" I shook the letter from home in Lucas's face. "My little sister Susie says it sounds like so much fun that she's going to join the Navy!"

Lucas didn't take her eyes off the page she was reading. "Yep," she mumbled. "You'd better save her before it's too late."

"But Susie's so stubborn," I said. "Ever since she was a little kid, she's been pigheaded. If you tell her to do something, she won't. If you tell her not to do something, she will."

"Well, then you'd better tell her to sign up right away before it's too late," Lucas suggested, moving her book up in front of her face to signal her disinterest in further conversation. I rapped my knuckles lightly on the back of her book.

"But what if she decides to take my advice for a change and then she signs up because I told her to and she hates it and it's all my fault?" I asked.

Lucas lowered her book enough to glare at me over the top of the page. "Make up your mind, pal," she said. "Either she listens to you or she doesn't. Besides, I thought you liked the Navy so much you were gonna be an admiral some day." She brought the book back up in front of her face.

"I'm having second thoughts," I admitted. "Look at us. We both got promoted to E-3. Big deal! Now we're Journalist Seamen instead of Journalist Apprentices." I flicked my finger disdainfully at the three little stripes on my left sleeve. "Three dinky little stripes—one for brewing sixty million gallons of coffee, one for filing a thousand tons of paper, and one for swabbing the stupid deck every day for a year." Lucas ignored me, so I raised my voice as I paced around the room, punching the dust particles silhouetted against the light from the window. "You'd think they could afford one little janitor out of the whole defense budget," I said, "but then they couldn't afford to buy so many flags to hang around the base so we'd have something to salute when we walk by."

"Knock it off, Johnson," Lucas interrupted. "You're just nervous about your exam scores. You always get depressed after you take a big test." We had just spent five hours taking the Navy-wide exams for advancement to petty officer. Every journalist in the Navy was in competition for the few promotions allotted to our specialty field.

"You study more than anyone I know," Lucas said. "You passed the test. Don't worry. In a few more months the results will be posted and you'll be a petty officer with an eagle on your arm just like the big kids. Now, tell me the truth. You like the Navy, don't you?"

"Ha!" I snorted.

"Come on."

"Well, I don't like standing duty," I said. "And I don't like being called a 'split-tail.' And I'm tired of wearing black shoes every single day. Why can't I wear a pair of pink shoes once in a while? I doubt if the national defense would suffer too much."

"Don't quibble with me, Johnson," Lucas said. "Forget about the duty and the gross sailors and the uniforms—what about the Navy? You like it, don't you?"

I nodded. She was right. I had to admit that, for some strange reason, I really did like the Navy and I enjoyed my work.

"Okay," Lucas said. "You like the Navy. Now can I read my book in peace?"

"I'm obviously a crazy person," I said, ignoring her request. "But we're talking about my baby sister. How can I tell her to join the Navy?" I kept pacing. "On the other hand, maybe it would be a good experience for her. I don't know what to tell her." I smacked myself on the forehead.

"I have a novel idea," Lucas offered. "Why not tell her the truth?" I stopped pacing and whirled to face her.

"That's it!" I exclaimed, clapping my hands. "We'll tell her the truth!"

"What do you mean 'we'?" Lucas looked at me out of the corner of her eye. "She's *your* sister."

"But I need your journalistic expertise for this project," I said, knowing that Lucas was very susceptible to flattery about her skill as a writer. She planned to spend four years in the Navy as a journalist and then return to Connecticut, where she'd be the ace reporter at her hometown newspaper. "We'll write her a guide to basic training—give her all the scoop straight from the poop deck, so to speak. Then she can make up her own mind and I won't be responsible. What a wonderful idea. You're so smart!"

"I know, Johnson. I know," Lucas sighed. "Can't you tell me something I don't know already, like how I let you talk me into wasting my free time writing guidebooks for dumb civilians who don't know any better than to join the service?" She tossed her novel down on her bed and looked at the ceiling, drumming her fingers on her knees. "Let's see. How about this: Am I military material, you may ask . . ."

Three hours later:

DISCLAIMER: THIS IS A COMPLETELY UNAUTHORIZED (BUT ABSOLUTELY TRUE) DOD PUBLICATION.

DISCOVER YOUR MILITARY POTENTIAL!

"Am I military material?" you may ask yourself during a TV commercial break one evening in this age of high unemployment and dwindling numbers of bachelors. Your job may seem dull compared to the jobs you see pictured in the Navy, where Every Job Is an Adventure. Or maybe you'd rather Be All That You Can Be in the Ar-ar-ar-my. And, of course, the Marines are always Looking for a Few Good Men, so why not join the manhunt?

Before you sign your life away, however, you want to be sure you have what it takes to be a member of our country's military forces. Do YOU, Ms. Ordinary Civilian, have true military potential?

The following 5-Step Test to Discover Your Military Potential is guaranteed to reveal your potential for military success in the comfort and privacy of your own home.

TEST #1 INSPECTION

Wearing just your underwear, stand in front of your refrigerator with the door wide open. Keep your arms straight down at your sides, heels together, toes pointed out at a 45-degree angle, and face straight ahead. Do not turn your head, scratch your nose, sneeze, cough, fart, burp, or make any other noise or movement. This unnatural position is called Attention.

This exercise will help you get the feel for standing outdoor inspections during the winter months. Since the most important aspect of standing inspection is to be able to ignore extreme cold and heat and other physical discomforts, if (disregarding your electric bill) you can tolerate this exercise for thirty minutes, you are definitely military material. (You should also see your doctor.)

TEST #2 MILITARY BEARING

Bearing is the ability to appear calm and untouched by havoc as it is wreaked right around your ears. Even if you don't join the service, Bearing is valuable for those who have children, teach school, or have a spouse/boyfriend who is prone to shouting.

Stand at Attention as in Step #1 (without the refrigerator). Have a friend stand uncomfortably close to you, peering with great interest at each detail of your body and clothing. Periodically, your friend should bring his or her face within three inches of yours and scream *"Quit eyeballing me, you worm! Cage those eyes. You aren't good enough to look at me, you slime!"* During the screaming, do not move your head or change your expression, even if your friend splashes little droplets of spit on your face.

The Inspecting Friend should remark that it looks like you comb your hair with a toilet-bowl brush and make other comments intended to ruffle you. Your job is to remain unruffled.

TEST #3 LET'S GET PHYSICAL

Let's test your physical condition, military style. Forget the jumping jacks and sit-ups—we're going to do The Hang.

Find a bar somewhere that is at least six feet off the ground. Jump or climb up and get a good grip on the bar with your palms facing towards your face. Hold yourself up, with your arms bent so that your chin is above (but NOT resting on) the bar. The object is to hang without straightening your arms, keeping your head well above the bar. This sounds simple, doesn't it? Try it.

Score yourself:

70 seconds—you'll love PT (physical training)

40–70 seconds—you will survive PT

Less than 40 seconds—maybe you'd rather sell Tupper-ware

TEST #4   COVERING YOUR HEAD

Tie a piece of wool around your forehead like a headband. Wear this on your way to work or while doing your housework. Wear it anytime you step out of doors during the day, even if you are just slipping out to get the mail or the newspaper.

Notice that your hair gets mashed down and a dorky-looking ridge appears around your head. You may also develop an unsightly rash or skin irritation from the scratchy material.

This test simulates wearing a military hat. Military people must always wear hats outdoors when in uniform (a regulation that is rumored to be based on the fact that most senior officers have very little hair, but very many shiny things on the fronts of their hats). Another reason for the covered head rule is that you must salute while wearing your hat. Saluting is a very popular pastime in the military service.

TEST #5   GROUP HYGIENE

This final test is designed to check your ability to perform personal hygiene in the presence of a group of strangers. You probably won't want to try this test with real strangers; instead, invite a group of female friends to your home for a unique party.

Have each person bring a toothbrush, soap, washcloth, towel, shower shoes, and pajamas. Inform your group that they have ten minutes to rush to the bathroom, brush their teeth, shower, put on their p.j.'s, clean the entire bathroom, and return to the living room. For a standard one-shower bathroom, you need a minimum of five people to get the proper effect.

Everyone must remove their clothes in the living room and crowd into the bathroom at the same time, standing in single file while waiting to shower, so they will feel very self-conscious. People are much more docile when they are naked, which is undoubtedly one of the reasons the military uses this tactic.

That's it! After completing these simple tests, you should have a very good idea of your natural military potential. The final, and most important, thing you should remember is: **DO NOT TAKE YOUR BRAIN WITH YOU TO BASIC TRAINING!** You will not need it. You will not use it. You stand a very good chance of having it washed if you take it with you. If this happens, you will end up reenlisting several times and will spend your entire working life wearing sturdy clothing, ugly shoes, and unattractive hairstyles, and eating faster than a speeding bullet.

"There! That ought to do it." I smiled to myself as I dropped the envelope into the mailbox, pleased that I had performed my sisterly duty. If Sue read our guidebook and still wanted to march a few miles in my oxfords, it would be her own decision.

A week later, I got another letter from Sue. She thanked me for the guidebook but said she wouldn't need it after all. She was getting married. Her boyfriend had proposed to her the day before she was scheduled to sign her enlistment contract.

I rushed into our cube. "Look at this!" I tossed the letter on Lucas's bunk. "Sue's getting married instead of joining the Navy. I can't believe it."

"What's so hard to believe?" Lucas asked. "Lots of women would rather be wives than Waves." She picked up Sue's letter and read it silently. "Like me, for instance."

I started to laugh, but the look on Lucas's face made me stop. "You're serious, aren't you?" I asked.

Lucas shrugged but didn't answer.

"I thought you liked traveling and meeting new people and having adventures."

"Oh, yeah," Lucas said. "It's a real adventure, living in a dump like this, isn't it?"

I glanced around our sparsely furnished cubicle, at the paint peeling off the register, the dents and scratches on our metal wall lockers, the worn gray blankets on our bunks. The room looked especially grim in the glare of fluorescent light from the overhead fixtures. "I guess the place could use a little interior decorating."

Ski stuck her head into the cube. "Looks like you're moving," she said. "Did you see the notice on the bulletin board downstairs?" I flew down the stairs. Ski was close behind. She tapped the notice.

"You'll be living in high style now," she said. "No more bus rides to work, no more cubicles, no more Hawkins."

"They didn't call me!" I said.

Ski snickered. "Why would they call a peon like you? Did you get promoted to base commander when I wasn't looking?"

For two months, I had stopped by every day to watch the construction of the new barracks. I asked so many questions that the foreman finally offered to call me personally if I would agree to leave his workers alone.

"Cement takes time to dry, sweetheart," he informed me one afternoon when I was being especially curious and pesky. "Girders take time to weld. And answerin' questions takes time that coulda been spent pouring cement or welding." He promised to call me if I would agree to stop interrupting his workers. I told Ski about our deal.

Ski rolled her eyes up towards the ceiling and threw her hands into the air. "You really believed he'd call you, didn't you, Johnson?" she laughed. "Haven't I taught you anything? You still go around believing everything people tell you." She followed me upstairs and into my cube, laughing all the way.

Lucas was standing in the midst of a pile of clothes and papers in the middle of the room. "I've been ready to leave this cell since the day I moved in here," Lucas said, grabbing a handful from the pile and stuffing it into her duffle bag.

"Hey, Lucas," Ski said. "You better sign up to room with Johnson. She still needs a baby-sitter."

"Be quiet," I said. Ski ignored me.

"Did you know she's been waiting for the construction foreman to call her and tell her that the barracks are ready?" she said. Lucas burst out laughing so hard that she lost her balance and tripped over her duffle bag. She fell on the floor, holding her sides and giggling. "Did she tell you that same story? I told her she was crazy, but she never pays any attention to me."

"Maybe the Chief of Naval Operations will call her personally and tell her she got promoted, too," Ski said. "He wouldn't want her to have to find out from reading the bulletin board like a normal person."

"Shut up!" I yelled. "There's nothing wrong with trusting people. You guys are always making fun of me, just because I believe people." They made me feel like a dumb hick. On the verge of tears, I said, "Maybe if you think I'm so stupid, you should just get a new roommate, Lucas!"

Lucas stopped laughing and sat up. "Aw, Johnson," she said. "We were only kidding. Don't get mad." She stood up and walked over to put her arm around my shoulder. "See what I mean? You believed us and we were only joking. We gotta be roommates, because we're best pals, right?" She gave me a big, goofy grin and wiggled her eyebrows up and down until I had to laugh.

"Okay," I said, still pouting.

"Besides," she added, punching me softly in the head, "I still gotta pay you back for that little trick in the club." She shook her head and gave me an evil look. "Making me pay for all those beers—that was the dirtiest trick you ever pulled on me, Johnson. But don't worry, I'll get you."

"Ha!" I said. "You think I believe that?"

"Geez, would you look at that building!" Lucas whistled softly. "Looks like a hotel or something."

The cream-colored stucco barracks shone amid the surrounding gray buildings. Six separate entrances led into the barracks, three on the ground floor and three upstairs. A smaller building in front of the barracks housed the visitors' lounge, laundry room, quarterdeck, and the Master-at-Arms's office. The MAA, Dora Braden, was a first-class petty officer with a leathery face and a no-nonsense personality, but she looked like a fairy princess compared to Hawkins.

"There must be real doors on the rooms in there," Lucas said, her voice hushed in admiration, as we lugged our bags up the stairs to the second deck.

There were doors, all right. The outer door opened onto a lounge with a color TV, red leather chairs, and a game table. Four more doors opened off the lounge.

"Ho! Ho! Look at this," Lucas chuckled. "Real beds. No more bunks. Pretty classy, huh?" She dumped her seabag on the bed nearest the window. I claimed the bed in the far corner of the room.

"If they give us another roommate, she can sleep by the door." Lucas nodded toward the third bed. "That way, if anyone breaks in, they'll get her first. Kind of like a human burglar alarm."

"You're such a thoughtful person," I said as I pulled my old stuffed rabbit out of my bag and propped him on my pillow. "Looks like home now, doesn't it?"

"Sure, Johnson," Lucas said. She pointed at a smaller door a few feet behind my bed. "What's in there?"

"Look at this!" I squealed. "A private bathroom with a real bathtub!" I turned both taps on full blast and began tearing my clothes off.

"What are you doing?" Lucas asked.

"What does it look like I'm doing?" I hopped into the tub. "I'm taking a bath." I sat down, enjoying the feel of the hot water swirling around me. "I haven't had a hot bath for a year. This is great!"

Shaking her head, Lucas walked into the other room.

"Lucas!" I suddenly yelled.

"What's the matter?" She rushed into the bathroom. "Are you okay?"

"I'm fine," I said. "But remember when you got assigned to stand the fire watch on the day you were supposed to go home for Christmas vacation?"

Lucas frowned. "You called me in here to discuss last Christmas while you take a bath?" Ignoring her sarcasm, I continued.

"Remember how I volunteered to stand your duty for you," I reminded her. "I didn't even charge you a penny and you said you owed me a big favor?" I raised my eyebrows and smiled sweetly.

"How could I forget?" Lucas sighed. "You remind me practically every day."

"Well, I won't remind you anymore, because I finally have a little favor to ask in return."

Silent, Lucas squinted her eyes and gave me an appraising look.

"Will you go over to the exchange and get me a bottle of bubble bath?" I asked.

"Are you kidding?"

"I'm serious! I *have* to have a bubble bath to celebrate our new barracks with our very own bathroom with a bathtub and a real door and a desk and an air conditioner," I explained. "This is a memorable day, Lucas. Please

please please please *please.*" Pride never kept me from begging when necessary.

"Okay," Lucas finally agreed. "But consider my debt paid in full."

"Yippee!" I smacked the water, spraying a small fountain across the bathroom floor. "You're a real pal!"

"I'm getting out of here before you soak me like you must have soaked your head, Johnson." Lucas shook her head and went back into the other room. When I heard her turn the doorknob, I called, "Oh, Lucas!" in my most innocent voice. Her sigh carried all the way into the bathroom.

"What is it *now*, Johnson?" she asked, resignedly.

"Stop at the package store and get some champagne on your way back."

"You know you're a crazy woman, don't you?" Lucas said.

"You betcha!" I screamed with glee.

"Okay, Johnson," she said. "I'll get you some bubble bath and some champagne, but that means you owe me a favor and you can't ask me to do anything for you again for at least six months."

"It's a deal!"

"You're crazy," Lucas repeated on her way out the door. "You're really crazy." The door slammed behind her, leaving me along in the luxury of a two-room suite with a ceramic-tile tub.

"No, I'm not." I stood up and saluted my reflection in the mirror across the bathroom. "I'm simply enjoying my military benefits."

Lucas returned about twenty minutes later, but she wasn't alone. A thin girl with big glasses and long, dark hair stood staring at me as Lucas handed me the bubble bath and the champagne. I smiled at the new girl, dumped the bubble bath into the water, and started swishing it around, making huge mounds of bubbles like they always have in the movies.

"McGrath," she said to the girl, "this is Johnson. She's crazy, but she's not dangerous." Lucas reached down and patted me on the head. "Just treat her like a normal person and try not to stare when she drools." Lucas then turned to me, "Johnson, this is our new roommate, Pat McGrath. Don't bite her, okay?"

I tossed a handful of bubbles into the air and directed a friendly bark in McGrath's direction. I thought she'd laugh, but she just gave me a funny look and left to accompany Lucas on her inspection of our new home.

I popped the cork and took a swig of champagne, choking as the bubbles exploded in my mouth. In between sputters, I called, "Anyone out there want a sip?" They pretended not to hear me, but I could hear them opening doors and moving furniture. "Look at this!" Lucas exclaimed, "We get little desks that fold down and our own chairs!"

"Look at these beds!" McGrath whispered. "They're made out of wood instead of metal and they're painted white. The bedspreads are even yellow! This is the prettiest place I've ever lived."

"She must have lived in an interesting house if it was uglier than a barracks," I muttered to myself.

"Well, I wouldn't go that far, McGrath," Lucas answered, "but it sure ain't bad for a barracks." McGrath said she was going downstairs to get the rest of her luggage. I jumped out of the tub and grabbed a towel. Peeking around the corner to make sure McGrath was gone, I whispered, "I don't know about that girl, Lucas. She sure looked at me funny. Gives me the creeps."

Lucas snickered and pointed at the bubble-covered champagne bottle in my hand. "Well, you have to admit that most people don't sit around in the bathtub in the middle of the day, drinking champagne and barking!"

I admitted that she had a point, but it didn't explain the funny feeling I got when McGrath was in the room. There was something about her that bothered me. "As Grandpa Carl Oscar Johnson used to say," I told Lucas, "it just don't set well with me."

McGrath was from upstate New York, Lucas explained, and had been raised by her grandmother after her parents were killed in a plane crash when she was a little kid. She had attended a strict all-girl school, run by nuns, and, apparently, was having a little trouble adjusting to her new surroundings. "She's okay," Lucas assured me. "She just needs some time to get used to Navy life."

"Why would anyone who was used to living around nuns join the Navy, I wonder," I said thoughtfully. "Seems like it would be too much of a shock."

"Yeah," Lucas agreed, "but maybe she thought it would be kind of the same because she still lives with a bunch of women."

McGrath was an intelligence specialist and worked the graveyard shift, so I didn't see much of her. But when she was around, she was always talking about what the nuns had taught her. The nuns said not to sit on the toilet seat. The nuns said not to trust men. The nuns said this and the nuns said that.

Most of the time, I ignored McGrath, but one night as I was polishing my toenails a glorious decadent red, she walked over and stared at my feet. "The nuns say that red nail polish is an invitation to the devil," she informed me in her wispy voice. I tried to keep my mouth shut, but the devil must have accepted the invitation to jump into my bottle of Forever Red Glamour Glaze, because I said, "Is that right? Well, I like red. And speaking of colors, do you know what's black and white and can't turn around in the hallway, McGrath?"

"No." She stared at me through her horn-rimmed glasses.

"A nun with a harpoon in her neck!" I screamed, slapping my knee and laughing hysterically. The joke wasn't funny. I knew that. In fact, I punched the sailor who had told me the joke. "That's really sick," I told him, but for some reason, I was compelled to tell McGrath the joke. She made a funny sound in her throat and burst into tears. I felt so bad.

Putting my arm around her shoulder, I said, "Hey, McGrath, don't cry. I know that wasn't a funny joke, I was just being mean." To my relief, she stopped sobbing. Then, abruptly, she threw both arms around my neck and wouldn't let go.

"Okay, McGrath," I said, ducking out from under her arms. "I gotta finish my nails now." She just sat there, giving me that funny stare of hers.

"You're exaggerating things, pal," Lucas insisted when I told her about McGrath hugging me. McGrath was in the bathroom, brushing her teeth.

I was already in bed, but I couldn't fall asleep. "She's so weird, Lucas," I whispered. Lucas was getting undressed for bed. She peeled off her socks, throwing one in the general direction of her laundry bag. She aimed the other one at my head.

"You're the one who's acting weird, Johnson," she pointed out. "The first time she met you, you barked at her. And only a person with a weird sense of humor would tell a poor Catholic orphan a gross joke about nuns. Now shut up and go to sleep."

"I can't sleep," I said. "I keep thinking about it."

"Think about something else, then," Lucas suggested. "Think about your hot date this weekend. That ought to occupy your little mind."

"Good idea," I said. The same sailor who told me the sick nun joke had promised to take me to a jazz festival in Washington, D.C., Friday night. Humming softly to myself, I finally fell asleep. Sometime in the middle of the night, I woke up, startled. I could sense someone's presence near my bed, but my eyes weren't accustomed to the dark and I couldn't see anything. Then, I felt a hand on my breast. I jumped up and turned on the light. McGrath was kneeling beside my bed, still wearing those homely glasses. I grabbed her wrist. "What do you think you're doing, McGrath?"

"Nuthin'," she whispered.

"Nuthin'!" I screamed. "You call grabbing my boob nuthin'?"

"What's going on?" Lucas sat up, rubbing her eyes. "What are you yelling about, Johnson?"

"McGrath grabbed my boob while I was sleeping. That's what I'm yelling about!" Tired, shocked, and confused, I started crying. "I told you she was weird."

McGrath stood up. "I'm not weird, Johnson," she said. "I just like you."

"Well, I'm not interested in a love affair with a girl!" I exploded. "If you ever touch me again, I'll break your arm. I mean it, McGrath! I'll break both your arms. And your legs, too!" I jumped out of bed and reached for her, but she ran over and jumped into her bed, drawing the covers up under her chin.

"Don't break her arms, Johnson," Lucas said calmly, unruffled as usual. "You'll get busted and you won't get to be a petty officer." She was right.

"Okay," I said. "But I want you out of this room,

McGrath. I'm going down and talk to Braden first thing in the morning."

"No!" McGrath screamed, shrinking back against her pillow. It was the first time she had ever spoken above a whisper. "They'll kick me out of the Navy and I don't have anywhere to go. I don't have a family or anything. Please, Johnson, I promise I won't ever touch you again." She looked like a scared little kid, hiding in her bed.

Heaving a big sigh, I sat down on the edge of my bed, holding my head in my hands. What a predicament! I didn't want to ruin the girl's life, but I sure didn't want to live with her, either. No one spoke for quite a long time. McGrath finally broke the silence.

"I have a friend who has an empty bunk in her room. She'll let me move in with her," she whispered, back to her normal voice. "Just promise you won't tell on me. Please. I'll ask Braden in the morning."

The next day, McGrath moved out, but I still had trouble falling asleep that night. I kept looking over at her empty bed.

"You did the right thing, pal," Lucas said, successfully reading my thoughts. "If she got kicked out of the Navy because of you, you'd never forgive yourself."

"Yeah, I guess so," I shrugged.

Lucas sat up halfway in her bed, resting her weight on one elbow. "How come you got so upset, anyway, Johnson?" she asked. "She probably wouldn't have bothered you again after the way you screamed at her."

It took a few minutes for me to sort out my thoughts and feelings well enough to put them into words.

"I don't know, Lucas," I finally answered. "All day long, I have to put up with smart remarks from the guys at work. And the sailors and Marines yell at every female who walks by on the street. When I come home, I want to feel safe and comfortable. I don't need someone in my own room making passes at me while I'm sleeping."

"Well, you're safe tonight, Johnson." Lucas rearranged her pillow and lay back down. "You're not my type."

"That breaks my heart."

"I know," Lucas said, "but I had to tell it to you straight. Good night, pal."

"Good night."

Just as I was about to drift off, I felt something touch my bed. Not again! I thought. McGrath is gone! What's going on here? I switched on the light as the head of my old stuffed rabbit came into view from beneath my bed.

"Oh, Johnson, I like you so much," a muffled voice said.

I kicked the rabbit as hard as I could.

"Ouch!" Lucas sat up, rubbing her arm. "You don't have to get violent!" she said.

"What in the world are you doing?" I demanded.

"I thought maybe you could use a little joke to cheer you up," she said, still rubbing her arm where I had kicked her. "You've been taking this whole thing so seriously."

"That was real thoughtful of you, Lucas," I said, unable to resist smiling any longer. She looked so ridiculous crawling around on the floor in her pajamas, holding a raggedy stuffed rabbit.

"Gee, pal!" she brightened. "Thanks! I knew you'd appreciate it."

"Oh, I really appreciate it," I said. "I appreciate it so much I'm going to think real, real hard of a way to make it up to you. Don't worry about that, Lucas."

"Wonder what made her think I was worried," Lucas muttered to the rabbit as she crawled back into bed.

9

Mean,
Green Machines

There was no doubt about the femininity of the girl who took McGrath's place as our roommate. Olson was a tiny blonde with a headful of curls and a suitcase full of electric hair rollers. I didn't see her very often because she worked in a different building and spent all her free time with a big, hairy Marine. I saw him come by to pick her up a couple of times. He looked like a bald gorilla, so I was content to keep my distance.

Marines were a fascinating new species. Except for the one who got beat up by the women in the barracks, the only Marines I'd seen up close were the ones at the gates, who were so stiff they looked like cardboard paper dolls, strutting around, saluting, and waving the cars on and off the base with their white gloves. I asked Chief Bagget why sailors didn't guard their own bases. He explained that Marines are actually in the Department of the Navy, though they hate to admit it, and have to be kept busy while they're waiting for the chance to use their finely honed combat skills. "The thing Marines like best is killing commies," the chief told me. "After that, their favorite hobbies are saluting, grunting, and running. A Marine's idea of a good time is running ten or fifteen miles in formation, singing killer songs."

Later that week, I saw some Marines running in formation. It was an unforgettable experience. Normally, I wasn't out and about at five A.M., but that morning I had just been relieved from duty when a platoon ran by, dressed in red shorts, yellow T-shirts, and combat boots, singing:

Issued me an M-16,
Turned me into a killing machine!
Issued me a hand grenade,
Shoulda seen the mess I made!

I'm a hard, green fighting machine,
I'm rough and tough, I'm lean and mean!
When I fire, I aim to kill.
If I don't get you, my buddy will!

Sound off—one, two
Sound off—three, four.
One, two, three, four
U.S. Marine Corps!
Ooh-rah!

It's the "Ooh-rah" that distinguishes the Marines from any other group of humans. They yell it with such malicious enthusiasm and at such a high decibel level that they scare the enemy to death, even if they don't shoot them. When there aren't any communist enemies available to fight with, the Marines fight with the sailors, just so they don't lose their touch. Marines call sailors titless Waves and sailors call Marines jarheads. The Marines say if God wanted you to be in the Navy, you'd have been born with webbed feet and tacky tattoos. And the sailors answer that if God wanted you to be a Marine, he would have given you the IQ of a rock and green, baggy skin.

"Why do the sailors and the Marines always pick on each other?" I asked the chief.

"It's kind of like teasing your mother," he answered. "You can pick on her all you like, but let a stranger try it and you'll kill him. You should see what happens if a civilian insults a sailor when there are Marines around. They whump him good."

Shortly after we moved to the new barracks, I had the opportunity to observe some Marines at close range. One morning at two A.M., the fire alarm went off and women spilled out of the barracks, wearing everything from nighties and T-shirts to raincoats and blankets. Before we could go back to bed, the MAA—the Master-at-Arms—had to take a roll call and make sure every female body was accounted for, which took quite a while. We stood outside in the nippy night air, hopping from one bare foot to the other, waiting for the firemen to check the building.

The enlisted men's barracks was directly across the street from ours, providing a wonderful view for the men hanging out of the windows, looking through binoculars, taking photos, and calling to us.

"Hey, sweetheart, if you're cold, you can come over and crawl in between my sheets!"

"Woowee! I wouldn't kick you out of bed for snoring, baby."

Their amusing remarks gave us something to concentrate on other than freezing to death while we waited to return to our warm beds, but when the MAA announced the next day that there hadn't been any threat of fire—just a fire drill, arranged by the Marines—their remarks didn't seem so amusing. It was understandable that they were anxious to check out their feminine neighbors, but it wasn't very considerate to expect us to put on an impromptu fashion show in the chilly pre-dawn.

Two nights later, the fire alarm shrieked again. This time, as we poured out of the barracks, it started to rain.

The novelty of standing outdoors in our pajamas had worn off and this time none of the women was amused by the men's chatter. Being forced to leave our warm beds to stand outdoors in the cold night was bad enough, but having to stand around in soggy pajamas really dampened our spirits.

Lucas was particularly upset because she had stood duty from six P.M. until two A.M. and had just fallen asleep when the alarm started its raucous clanging.

"My brother was right," she muttered, as a truckful of Marines armed with machine guns and wearing helmets screeched into the parking lot. They jumped off the truck and rushed to their posts around the building although they knew darned well there was no fire.

"My brother said Marines get their heads shaved when they enlist because the doctors don't want any hair in the way during the brain surgery," Lucas said as we watched their display of fire-fighting readiness. "The doctors perform frontal lobotomies on all the recruits. Then the Marines keep their heads shaved so they can check periodically to make sure that not even one little smidgen of brains has grown back." She didn't bother to speak quietly, even though she knew that Marines get violent if someone insinuates that they are anything less than brilliant military strategists.

"Is that right, Wave?" asked a beefy young man dressed in camouflage greens who was standing behind us.

"Yeah," Lucas snapped in return.

"Well, I hear that a girl can't join the Waves unless she's so ugly it looks like her face caught fire and someone put it out with a rake," he countered.

"Oh yeah?" Lucas was warming up. "Well, I heard that they sew the butts shut on all you grunts, so that after twenty years, you'll be so full of shit you'll explode and they won't have to pay you any retirement money. That's why the Marine Corps is so cost effective, saving all those defense dollars."

The Marine stood glaring at Lucas, hitting his nightstick against his palm, trying to decide whether to smack Lucas, when his platoon sergeant walked by.

"Got a problem here, Private?" he growled.

The private gave Lucas one last dirty look, rammed his stick back into his utility belt, and stalked off into the night.

In the chow hall the next morning, Olson and her hirsute friend shared a table with me and Lucas. As soon as she finished her breakfast, Olson rushed off to work with King Kong in tow. Before we had a chance to stand up, two Marine privates marched over to the table, looking very spiffy in their crisp khaki shirts and blue pants with the little red stripes down the seams. "Would you ladies mind if we join you?" one of them asked politely. Their name tags identified them as Privates Martin and Carter.

"Here, let me take that tray back to the kitchen for you," Carter said, picking up the heavy tray with one hand so that we could fully appreciate his bulging biceps.

After a few minutes of idle chitchat, the two Marines looked at each other and nodded. Martin said, "Hey, aren't you the Wave that was giving Private Boucher a hard time at the fire drill last night?" They obviously knew it was her, so Lucas didn't bother to deny it.

"Yeah, that was me," she said. "I was just kidding, but I guess he doesn't have much of a sense of humor. Let's just forget the whole thing." She smiled and started to stand up, but Carter put his hand on her shoulder and shoved her back down in the chair. She landed with a thud.

The tables in the chow hall were very close together, so

the people seated nearby were undoubtedly listening, but Martin seemed to enjoy the attention.

"That's a good idea," he said. "Let's forget the whole thing and be friends. I hear Waves are real friendly." He looked at Carter. "Didn't you hear that Waves are *real* friendly, Carter?" Carter nodded his head and grinned.

"Yeah," he said. "I heard that when Waves go to basic training they have a special operation done on their feet to give them round heels. Then, a guy just has to push one lightly and she falls on her back, with her legs apart, and smiles." Carter still held Lucas's shoulder, so she didn't say a word, but I wasn't about to take that kind of insult from anybody.

"Eat my shorts, jarhead!" I hollered as I jumped to my feet, shoved Carter out of the way, and pulled Lucas out of her chair. I didn't know precisely what "eat my shorts" meant, but I had heard a sailor say it to a Marine and the phrase had a nice spit-in-your-eye ring to it. Our fellow diners dropped any pretense of not eavesdropping and turned to stare at the two privates as, noses high in the air, Lucas and I marched out of the dining hall. Everyone in the room laughed and turned to stare at the two privates. Marines hate to look foolish almost as much as they hate communists.

"I ought to hit you with my nightstick, you dumb bitch," Martin said, catching up to us outside the chow hall.

"Okay, hit us," I jeered. "Marines are supposed to be really tough. Must have got that reputation from beating up on women. Ooh!" Instead of looking embarrassed, as I thought he would, Martin grabbed his nightstick and would have smashed me if I hadn't started running.

Chief Bagget met me at the door to the office. "What's your hurry?" he asked. "I didn't know you were so anxious to get to work in the morning."

I told him about the fire drills and our confrontation at breakfast. "Don't mess with those Marines, Johnson," the chief advised after hearing my story. "They're trained to fight and most of them don't care if you're a man or a woman. If you challenge them or make fun of the Corps, they'll knock the stuffing out of you." He handed me a stack of messages.

"Here," he said. "Think you can manage to deliver these to the Old Man's office without running into any Marines?"

Admiral Danworthy's office was on the third deck of the building. To get there, I had to cross the elaborate quarter-deck. Flags and paintings of Naval ships at sea decorated the walls, interspersed with framed awards and silver, engraved plaques. In the center of the floor were some colored tiles in the shape of an eagle, surrounded by a ring of letters which spelled out some nifty Latin saying that I never could remember. I liked to pretend it said *Non illegitimus carborundum*, which roughly translates to "Don't let the bastards wear you down." The admiral's office was across the eagle and up two flights of skinny little stairs.

I tried to avoid the quarterdeck whenever possible, because Admiral Danworthy, otherwise known as Dan the Dragon, had a reputation as a pretty stern character. The one time I ever saw him walking around like ordinary people, he had paid a surprise visit to the chow hall. Everyone stopped chewing to stare at him as he strolled through, nodding at his subjects and noting a cracked counter here and a dirty table there. On his heels, his aide carried a clipboard on which he duly noted all discrepancies.

The admiral and his entourage left the chow hall just before I did, so I was close behind as he skirted the hat rack on his way out the door. He reached up and grabbed a commander's cap from the rack. "This cover is filthy," he said. "Absolutely unacceptable for a naval officer." The hat looked fine to me, but an admiral undoubtedly has had more experience inspecting for dirt than a mere seaman has. He tossed the hat to his ever present aide and asked, "Who owns this piece of garbage?"

"It appears to belong to Commander Byrd, sir," the aide replied, reading the name on the label inside the hatband.

"Have Commander Byrd report to my office at 0700 tomorrow, with a haircut and a new cover," Admiral Danworthy barked.

I did a quick about-face and marched back into the chow hall. If the admiral ordered a commander who had a speck of dirt on his hat to get a haircut and a new cover, I could just imagine how he'd react to the sight of my dingy hat. He'd probably order me to shave my head and bury my hat at sea.

As I crossed the quarterdeck entrance to the admiral's office, my footsteps echoed in the early-morning silence. The third deck was as deserted as the rest of the building, so I dropped the messages on the admiral's yeoman's desk and started back down the stairs.

When I was a kid, I used to lean down, hold both railings, and see how many steps I could jump over. The admiral's stairs were so short that I couldn't resist the temptation to try for a complete leap, a feat I had never accomplished as a child. I grabbed the banister, walked my hands halfway down the flight, and jumped, keeping my eye on the floor at the bottom of the stairs, where I hoped to land. I made it all the way to the bottom and landed on my feet!

As I straightened up, I found myself belly-to-belly with Admiral Danworthy. He had apparently walked quietly across the quarterdeck and stood watching me perform gymnastics on his stairs. He didn't say a word, just looked at me, quizzically. Fear paralyzed me for a few seconds.

Recovering, I snapped to attention and saluted. "Good morning, sir!"

I took off for my office on the run, hoping the admiral hadn't had time to read my name tag. I was sure I'd pushed my luck too far and this would be the day that the MPs came to get me. They would probably understand my fighting with Marines, but there had to be an article in the regulations which prohibited touching an admiral's stomach.

Each time the phone rang during the day, I turned another shade whiter, positive that it was the admiral's aide calling to report me. By mid-afternoon, I was so pale and had spent so much time in the head that Chief Bagget, convinced that I was seriously ill, sent me home early. Anxious to leave before he had a chance to reconsider and change his mind, I grabbed my purse and ran outside. The phone rang as I closed the office door, but I pretended not to hear Chief Bagget calling to me.

Behind the locked doors of the barracks, I finally relaxed, certain that I was safe, at least until the morning. I took a hot shower to calm my nerves and had just crawled into bed for a quick nap when Lucas burst into the room.

"Hey, Johnson," she said. "There's some man down on the quarterdeck looking for you." I shot out of bed. Dan the Dragon must have tracked me down!

"Tell him I'm not here," I said as I looked around for a place to hide.

"He knows you're here, Johnson," Lucas said, kicking off her shoes and throwing her jacket on the bed. "I heard the MAA tell him she saw you come in a little while ago."

"Tell him I'm too sick to come downstairs," I said, climbing into my locker. The door wouldn't shut all the way, so I climbed back out and tried to crawl under the bed. Lucas stopped undressing and stood staring at me, her pants around her ankles and her shirt half off.

"What's the matter with you, pal?" she asked. "You're acting like a maniac." I ran over and grabbed Lucas by the shoulders.

"You gotta help me," I pleaded. I quickly told her about hitting the admiral in the stomach. "Please go down and tell the guy I'm not here. I promise I'll never ask you to do anything for me again, as long as I live. Cross my heart and hope to spit and die."

"Okay, pal," Lucas shrugged, pulling her uniform back on. "I'll tell the man you're not here. But after that, you're on your own. I'm not messing with any admirals."

Before I had time to plan my escape, she was back upstairs, her face looking grim.

"He wouldn't buy my story, Johnson," she said, in a hushed voice. "This guy is tough. Must be in the secret police. I think you better come downstairs. If you don't he'll probably come up here and shoot the door down." She glanced over her shoulder as if she expected to see him come crashing through the door that very second.

"You're kidding!" I couldn't believe it. All I did was *touch* an admiral, I didn't hurt him. "Does he have a gun?"

"I'm pretty sure he does," Lucas said. She walked over and patted me on the arm. "Don't worry, pal, I bet they'll just arrest you to scare you, the way they do little kids who steal cheap toys from dime stores."

"Okay," I sighed, taking one last look around the room at my familiar belongings in case they put me in the brig for a few years.

"I'll walk downstairs with you, pal," Lucas offered. "It's the least I can do."

A man dressed in blue stood with his back to the door, talking to Braden.

"There's Johnson." She nodded towards me as Lucas held the door and gently shoved me inside. He turned around, picked up his yellow hard hat off the counter, and smiled. "Hello, there. I was just over here checking the wiring in one of the rooms and I thought I'd stop by and make sure you approve of this new building." Speechless, I stared at the construction foreman with my mouth hanging open. Apparently, he mistook my silence for a reproach.

"I would of called like I promised," he said, "but I got busy and clean forgot." I finally found my voice.

"That's okay," I said, grabbing his hand and pumping it up and down wildly. "Thanks for stopping by. Thanks a lot. I really appreciate it."

"No problem." He donned his hard hat. "Well, I better get back on the job. You know how easy it is to distract those boys from their work." He winked and touched his fingers to the brim of his hat in a mock salute. Turning to the MAA, he nodded, "Thanks, ma'am," and sauntered out the door. As he walked out of sight, I realized that Lucas had purposely scared me because I'd been right all along about trusting the foreman. I turned around to tell her what I thought of her dirty trick, but she had disappeared.

"I'm going to kill you right now," I said, walking towards Lucas. She backed up, putting her hands out to keep me at a distance.

"You have to admit it was a good one," she said, backing into her bed. "You really fell for it." I walked onto her bed, still reaching for her as she scrambled to her feet on the other side.

"I'm going to kill you," I repeated in a monotone, my eyes bulging, as I flexed my fingers and continued walking slowly toward her. There was no way out. I was between

Lucas and the door. She ran into the bathroom. I followed her and yanked the door open so that it banged loudly against the wall.

"Come on, pal." Lucas laughed nervously and backed up against the tub. "Knock it off. Quit acting so spooky. I'm sorry I said you were dumb for believing people, okay?" She climbed into the tub and pressed up against the wall. "I'm sorry I told you he was a policeman. Come on, pal."

"I'm going to kill you," I repeated as I lunged for her neck.

"Johnson!!!" she screamed, raising her arms in front of her face. Reaching up, I turned on the cold water full blast, aiming the shower at her head.

"You didn't really think I'd kill you, did you?" I laughed as I closed the sliding door and held it so she couldn't get out. "You should know better than to believe everything people tell you."

Chief Bagget said I didn't look sick, so he wouldn't let me go to morning sick call. He said if I still felt bad, I could go in the afternoon.

"It may be too late by this afternoon, Chief," I told him.

"Why, do you have something immediately terminal?" He felt my forehead. "You don't have a temperature. You have rosy cheeks, bright eyes, and a clear complexion." Sitting back down at his desk, he rested his chin in his hand and grinned at me. "Maybe that wig is cutting off the circulation to your brain."

I'd sneaked quietly into the office a little early that morning, in the futile hope that, if I were busy working, no one would notice the blond wig—courtesy of Olson—I was wearing in anticipation of that morning's meeting with Admiral Danworthy. Our entire staff had been summoned to the admiral's cabin for an awards ceremony because of the excellent job we'd done arranging the base participation in the annual Azalea Festival. I didn't think Admiral Danworthy would be apt to make the connection between a curly-haired blonde and the brown-haired seaman who had recently greeted him, belly-to-belly, on the quarterdeck.

I struck a glamor girl pose and breezily answered, "I just thought a change in hair color might add a little excitement to my life, Chief."

"I'd have thought that being personally congratulated by an admiral would be enough excitement for one day," the chief replied. As our staff assembled in the waiting room outside the admiral's office, he whispered, "You'll be real glad you didn't miss this."

A large American flag stood in the corner of the room. I paced back and forth, casually getting nearer to the flag. I figured the flag was big enough for me to hide behind if I could just maneuver myself into the corner, but Chief Bagget was on the alert. He made me sit down and had just begun a most interesting lecture on the merits of proper military bearing when the office door swung open.

"Attention on deck!" the chief bellowed and everyone jumped to their feet. The admiral launched immediately into his speech, which I was too nervous to appreciate. As he ended with, "Your superior performance brings great credit to yourselves, this command, and the U.S. Navy. I personally commend each of you for a job well done." I breathed a sigh of relief, thinking I would soon make my escape. But, instead of giving the command to "carry on," the admiral started walking down the line, stopping to chat with each individual and distributing the award citations. Each award was accompanied by a grip and a grin. The admiral smiled and shook hands with the recipient, as the staff photographer recorded the moment for posterity.

By the time the admiral reached my position at the end of the line, I could feel the perspiration-soaked wig slipping slowly to the side of my head. I cocked my head and held my breath, hoping to stop the wig from slipping further, as he approached. My posture must have made Admiral Danworthy seasick, because he cocked his head slightly as he shook my hand, looked me in the eye, and said, "Well done, Seaman Johnson." I wasn't wearing my nametag that morning. I had ducked into the head and sneaked it into my pocket on the way to the ceremony, hoping it would make me less conspicuous.

"You have a wonderful memory, sir," the chief remarked, "remembering all the names of the people on your staff the way you do. You haven't met Seaman Johnson before."

"Oh, we met earlier this week," the admiral replied. "This young lady made quite an impression on me." He turned and strode into his office without another word.

"What did you do to impress Admiral Danworthy?" the chief asked as we left the admiral's cabin.

"I don't know, Chief," I said, as I daintily walked down the same stairs that I had jumped down just a few days earlier. "He must have been impressed by my military bearing."

10

The
Gofer Girls

From the window of Chief Bagget's office, I could see a
sailor strutting up the gangplank of the USS *Forrestal*,
his seabag slung over his shoulders. "Look at him," I said.
He paused, saluted the flag and tossed his bag on deck,
then turned to wave good-bye to someone on the pier. He
could have been waving to me.

I nodded towards the ship. "He's off to some interesting
place and I'm still here, filing boring papers." I thumped
the side of the file cabinet with my fist, forgetting that it
was made of steel. "Ouch!" Sucking on my hand, I flopped
down in the chair next to Chief Bagget's desk.

"Tsk! Tsk! Tsk!" The chief patted me on the head. "All
those sailors out at sea wanting to come home while poor
little ungrateful you doesn't appreciate walking on dry
land." He rolled his eyes. "What's the matter? Don't you
like your job here?"

"I like it fine, Chief." I knew he was only teasing, because he was a salty chief petty officer. He couldn't admit
that he liked me and might actually miss me if I left.
"You're the finest sailor I've ever seen and I really appreciate all the things you've taught me, Chief." I restrained
myself from patting his bald head. "Remember the first
day I reported for work? You took one look at me, put your
hands on your hips, stroked your beard, shook your head,

and said, 'Uh-uh. You won't last a week without my help.' "
We both laughed.

"I was right, wasn't I?" Chief Bagget asked.

"As usual," I said. "But that was over a year ago and I'm still just a gofer. I go fer coffee, I go fer messages, I go fer the trash detail. The farthest I've traveled is from this filing cabinet to the coffee room." This time, I kicked the cabinet. My hand still ached from punching it.

"Here. Take a trip," Chief Bagget snickered, handing me his empty coffee mug.

"See what I mean?" I grumbled. I took the cup and hurried down the hall to the coffee room and back, anxious to continue our discussion.

"Adventures, education, and travel—that's what the Navy's all about, Chief," I said as I set the steaming mug down on his desk. "I'm getting educated. I've been taking college classes on base ever since I got here." Chief Bagget nodded as he sipped his coffee. "But I still haven't had any adventures or travels. I can't wait too much longer before I get going. Jeepers! I'm already almost twenty-one years old and I haven't been anywhere!" I flopped down into the chair in front of his desk and propped my chin on my fists, giving him a soulful look.

The chief slapped his cheek. "Well! We'd better think of something fast," he said, "before senility strikes."

"Come on, Chief," I pleaded. "I'm serious. Can't you think of some way for me to get a travel assignment?" He stroked his beard for a minute, then walked over and pulled a thick manual from the shelf above the filing cabinet.

"Let's see," he said, as he thumbed through the pages. "Here we are. Just like I thought, there's a couple of specialties in the journalist rating. You could be a broadcaster. All those billets are either on board ship or overseas." I sat up.

"You mean they have broadcasters in the Navy?" I asked. "Real ones, like on radio and TV?"

Chief Bagget marked his spot in the book with his finger and looked up with a smile. "We even have real radio and TV stations called the American Forces Radio and Television Service," he said. "Unofficially, we call them A-FARTS. They broadcast news and entertainment to U.S. troops overseas where the people either don't speak English or the government censors all the media."

I jumped to my feet and cupped my left hand over my ear. Grabbing the chief's stapler in my right hand, I held it in front of my mouth. "Good morning, ladies and gentlemen and all the ships at sea," I said. "This is Navy broadcaster LouAnne Johnson bringing you the latest scoop, hot off the newswire!" Already, I could picture myself broadcasting the news headlines to my fellow Americans in some exotic foreign port. "We bring a special live report this morning from Chief Bagget, the most outstanding sailor on the staff of the Supreme Allied Commander Atlantic. Whaddya say, Chief?" I held the stapler under his nose.

"You'd better sit down here and make a list," he said, and pointed to the chair. "You have a little bit of work to do before you get your million-dollar contract." He read the requirements from the manual and I wrote down the list of forms I needed to get from the personnel office.

"Personal History Form, Performance Appraisal, Security Clearance, Background Investigation, Request for Transfer, Certificate of Eligibility." I read my list. "Do they want a note from my mommy, too?"

"Nope," Chief Bagget said, as he closed the book. "But they do want an audition tape."

"That'll be fun," I said, bouncing in my chair. "I can use the recording studio where we tape the NATO press releases, can't I?"

"You can use the studio," he said, "but you'd better settle down and get serious. There aren't many seats in that class. The competition will be tough." He took a sip of coffee, giving me an appraising look over the top of his cup. "You're a female, too," he added.

"What's that got to do with it?"

"Well, you should know. You've been there," he said. "Them good old boys at Fort Ben ain't exactly women's libbers."

"Fort Ben!" I cried.

"Fort Ben!" Lucas cried. "You said you'd never go back there alive. Isn't that what you said when we left, pal?" She picked up a stone near the dock and tossed it into the water. Two aircraft carriers had returned to Norfolk that afternoon and we had gone down to admire the mammoth gray vessels along the piers.

"Yeah, Lucas," I said. I sat down and dangled my feet over the edge of the dock. "But that was before I found out that we could go back there to learn to be radio and TV broadcasters."

Lucas fired another stone into the water, scaring a flock of sea gulls. "Did you forget about Sergeant Burke?" she shouted as the birds rose in a squawking cloud. "She remembers us, I betcha."

"Chief Bagget called up to check on that," I said. "Sergeant Burke volunteered to be a drill instructor at Army basic training so she could pick on the helpless new recruits for a while."

Lucas walked over and squatted next to me for a minute. "You've got all the answers, haven't you, pal?" she asked, then stood up and paced a few steps. She turned around. "I like it here. Look how pretty it is with the ocean and the beaches and ships." She waved her arms towards the ocean, where the sun was setting and strings of little white lights illuminated the gangways and portholes of the ships. The lights reflected on the waves lapping gently at the dock. "We finally got a nice room at the new barracks, too," Lucas added.

I drummed my feet against the wooden piling beneath the dock. "Come on, Lucas!" I cried, exasperated. "You could have stayed at home if you only wanted a nice room. The Navy's the place to *travel* and get educated."

"We're getting educated," Lucas said. "The GI Bill is paying for our college."

"That's exactly my point! Now is our chance to travel!"

"How many miles do you have to go?" Lucas asked. "You traveled from Pennsylvania to Orlando for basic training. Then you traveled all the way here to Norfolk." I jumped up and grabbed her shoulders.

"Will you be serious!" I shouted. "I could shake you until your teeth rattle. I'm talking about *exotic* places. Don't you want to travel to foreign lands like the sailors on these ships?" I pointed at the aircraft carriers, destroyers, and mine sweepers in front of us. "Don't you want to meet natives and eat interesting foods and see other cultures?"

A carload of sailors drove by, slowing to roll down the windows and whistle. "How about those natives," Lucas nodded at the car. "Aren't they interesting enough for you?"

"Whee! Hel-lo, baby! Whaddya say, sweetheart?" the sailors shouted.

I quit shaking Lucas and moved over to stand beside her, our elbows locked. "Ready, slouch," I whispered. We let our shoulders droop and pushed our bellies out, then tucked our bottom lips under our front teeth. Waving at the astonished sailors, we launched into a tune my sister Sue had taught me:

> We are the gofer girls,
> We really go fer guys.
> They never go for us,
> We always wonder why!

As we ended the verse, we smacked our front teeth up and down against our lower lips, producing a singularly unattractive sound. The windows of the car were rolled up in a flash and the car squealed off into the night. We dropped to the dock, shaking with laughter. That song never failed to discourage unwanted attention.

"Was it something I said?" Lucas asked, fluttering her eyelashes.

"Naw," I said. "They probably figured two gorgeous creatures like us already had hundreds of boyfriends." I stood up and brushed the dirt off my pants. "You still didn't answer my question," I reminded Lucas. "Don't you want to travel?"

Lucas drew her knees up to her chest and wrapped her arms around her legs. She frowned at the waves breaking against the dock for a long time before she answered. "I don't know, pal," she said. "I'd like to go, but I don't have enough time left on my enlistment. I only have two years more. I'd have to sign up for another two-year hitch if I went to broadcasting school. That's too much of my young life to sacrifice for the good of my country." Shaking her head, she stood up and turned to me.

"You're the lifer, Johnson," she said. "You go be a TV star. I'll watch you from my easy chair after I get home from my job at the newspaper, where I won't have to take orders from morons and wear ugly clothes and put on a dumb hat every time I go outside." She pulled her hat down so her ears stuck out straight and grinned at me. I knew she was trying to make me laugh, but I didn't feel like smiling.

"We've been best pals since boot camp," I said. "We should stick together."

"Don't worry, pal." She patted my back. "We'll write letters and visit each other."

"Promise?" I asked.

Lucas bared her teeth and poked me in the chest with her finger. "Don't forget I still owe you one for making me think you were gonna kill me and then blasting the shower on my head," she threatened. "We'll see each other again."

I gave her a dubious frown.

"Cross my heart and hope to spit!" She made the familiar gesture. "I always pay my debts, don't I?"

"Yeah, I guess you do," I said with a sigh, finally accepting the fact that she wasn't going to share my new adventure. "But I'll miss you. You know you're just like a sister to me. If I go back to DINFOS by myself, I won't have anybody to talk to."

"You'll be fine, pal," Lucas punched me in the shoulder again. "Besides, I recall an Army sergeant who would be real happy to keep you company, I betcha."

"You mean Daniels?" I asked, as I sat back down on the edge of the dock.

"Of course," she said, plopping down beside me. "You had the hots for him at journalism school. You can't fool me."

I really did like Daniels, from the moment we ran into each other—literally—at Fort Ben. I'd left Chief Hatch's office, in tears over one of his cruel insults, and walked smack into a tall, slim Army sergeant with curly black hair and dangerous blue eyes.

"Whoa!" he said, with a slight twang. "Looks like you've been talking to Chief Hatch."

"Yeah," I sniffed. "How did you know?"

"I've been here for a spell." He winked and took my elbow, guiding me into the office he had just left. "Come over here and sit down for a minute," he said, indicating a chair. "There's a box of tissues on my desk. I'll be right back." I blew my nose and was inspecting the little plaque on his desk that read Sergeant J. Daniels, Administration Specialist, when he returned and sat down on the other side of the desk, grinning at me.

"Feeling better?" he asked. I shook my head and he started right in, making small talk. He told me he handled all the records for journalism students at the school office. "Handing out tissues to pretty ladies isn't one of my regular duties, but in your case I'll make an exception," he said with such a mischievous look that I had to smile. After that, he often invited me into his office to visit. We'd sit and swap stories about his brothers and his crotchety old grandma back in West Virginia and my grandpa "Pickle Puss" Johnson and the assorted siblings and relatives back in Pennsylvania. We both missed our families and enjoyed having someone special to talk to. I hated to leave Daniels when I finished journalism school, but he was in the Army and I was in the Navy and that was that.

Thinking about Daniels made me happy and sad at the same time. "You know I like Daniels a lot, Lucas," I said. "But if I see him again, I'll fall madly in love with him and then it'll break my heart when I have to leave."

"Naw." Lucas shook her head emphatically and nudged me with her elbow. "When you leave DINFOS, you'll go overseas and you'll be too busy appreciating exotic foreign cultures to be lonely." She smiled at me with her mouth, but the rest of her face looked sad as she softly said, "I wish you fair winds and following seas, pal."

We both turned back to watch the last glimmer of light disappear into the ocean, unwilling to face each other, or the fact that we both knew lots of military friends who had lost track of each other—even those who crossed their hearts and hoped to spit that it wouldn't happen to them.

11

Broadcast
Wave

GOOD MORNING AND WELCOME TO THE MORNING RE-
PORT. I'M NAVY JOURNALIST LOUANNE JOHNSON AND I'll
BE BACK WITH THE LATEST NEWS HEADLINES AND A
LOOK AT THE WEATHER AFTER THIS ANNOUNCEMENT.
(MUSIC STARTS.)

IT HURTS WHEN YOU GET RUN OVER BY A CAR, ESPE-
CIALLY IF YOU ARE NOT RIDING INSIDE ANOTHER CAR.
EVEN IF YOU ARE RIDING IN ANOTHER CAR, IT HURTS
MUCH WORSE IF YOU AREN'T WEARING A SEAT BELT. IN
FACT, IF YOU AREN'T WEARING A SEAT BELT, YOU COULD
FLY UP AND SQUASH YOUR HEAD ALL OVER THE INSIDE
OF YOUR WINDSHIELD. (MUSIC SWELLS, CYMBALS
CRASH.)

ANOTHER GOOD REASON TO WEAR YOUR SEAT BELT IS
THAT IF YOU GET CAUGHT RIDING AROUND ON BASE
WITHOUT ONE, THE MP'S WILL LOCK YOU UP AND TAKE
AWAY YOUR BIRTHDAY.

SO, WEAR YOUR SEAT BELTS, OKAY, FOLKS? (MUSIC
FADES.)

Dear Pal,
  That's how I start the radio news here at good old
DINFOS. You wouldn't recognize this place. The bar-
racks where we used to live is an armory now, so all the
students live on the other side of base, which means we
have to walk over a mile to get to school when it's 300
below zero in the mornings. But there are some good

146

changes, too. They've integrated us Navy types among the Army, Air Force, and Marines. I think it's a good idea for students of the inferior services to have a chance to live among the Navy troops. I always was a liberal.

But here's the BIG change: The barracks are now coed!!! I kid you not. The Army has really gone modern. Every other room in my hallway has real, live male *students living in it! Of course, there are three hundred and seventeen Army rules and regulations designed to take the fun out of this potentially interesting situation.*

There isn't much time for hanky panky, anyway, but I don't have to tell you that. I'm sure you remember how they pile on the homework here. And I've kind of volunteered as a tutor—for a baby Marine, no less! Private Billy Kuchera is only seventeen years old and oh-so-proud to be a U.S. Marine. (Ooh-rah!) He can do the homework, but sometimes the pace is a little too fast for him. Naturally, he refuses to raise his hand and ask questions in class. He doesn't want people to think Marines are dumb, so he keeps his mouth shut and flunks. It makes sense to him, I guess.

Anyway, Kuchera lives next door to me and one night I offered to help him with his homework and it just became a habit. I don't mind going over everything twice because I'm determined to be an honor student this time, partly to show Chief Hatch (the fat old fart is still here) that a woman can do it and partly because I want to be able to choose my duty station. It sure won't be easy, because we have a smaller class, so only the top student gets honors. But you know how I love a challenge.

Well, it's time to go study with Billy Boy, so I'll say "So long" for now. Give my regards to Ski and Chief Bagget and send me a letter soon.

GOOD EVENING,
NAVY JOURNALIST LOUANNE JOHNSON,
REPORTING

P.S. I almost forgot to tell you congratulations! I saw your name on the promotion list and I'm sure you saw mine. We did it! Pretty soon, we'll be official petty officers. Journalist Third-Class Johnson—sounds good to me.

P.P.S. I was gonna pretend that I didn't find out about your sneaky letter to Daniels, which you signed with MY name—but I didn't want you to think you were smart enough to get away with it. When I got to the base, Daniels was waiting for me with a dozen red roses. I was a little confused until he mentioned the letter I had written, telling him how much I looked forward to renewing our "friendship." Lucky for you he's such a hunk. Otherwise, I'd have you put to death for forging my name.

So, I owe you a good one, don't I, pal? Don't worry. When I get to the Philippines (this time I just know I'm going there), I'll try to find something special to send you to show my overwhelming appreciation for your thoughtfulness.

Kuchera and I had spent over three hours writing the script for his first television mini-feature. He finally came up with an idea for the ending when his roommate, Crawford, stomped into my room. Crawford wasn't very big, but what he lacked in height, he made up for in cockiness. He crossed his arms and leaned against the metal post of the bunk beds near the door.

"Kuchera, get your ass downstairs ASAP and square away your uniform for tomorrow," he bellowed. Kuchera bit his lip and frowned, still concentrating on the papers spread across my desk. "I'll be down in a little while, Crawford," he said, without lifting his eyes. "I just want to finish this paragraph."

Crawford stalked over and swept the papers off the desk. In the process, he knocked Kuchera's soda can over and the sticky liquid bubbled over the edge of the desk, splattering the precious pages that Kuchera had painstakingly written. "I said get your ass down there now!" Crawford hollered, ignoring the mess he had created. "I don't want you keeping me up all night, screwing around with

148

your gear." Kuchera and I scrambled around on the floor, trying to save as many papers as we could from landing in the soda.

Crawford was such a meatball. Only a few days earlier, he had kept every student in the barracks awake all night. In celebration of the winter's first snowfall, he filled his laundry bag full of snowballs. Then, in full combat gear, he ran down the hallways, screaming the Marine Corps yell. I was asleep, taking a peaceful walk through the countryside back home, and the sound crept into my dream as the bellowing of a bull charging across the pasture. Instead of a bull, Crawford charged into my room, stuffed a snowball into my pajamas, and ran out screaming. He worked his way up and down every hall in the building until he ran out of snowballs. His victims were either too sleepy or too busy trying to dry their clammy pajamas to bother chasing him.

"Well, if it isn't Private Snowball!" I said to Crawford as I crawled out from under the desk with one of the few dry sheets of paper. "You're a fine one to talk about keeping people awake. Why don't you leave us alone? We're almost finished." Kuchera didn't say a word. He was busy spreading the soggy pages across my bunk and trying to dry them off without smearing the ink.

"Shut up, bitch," Crawford growled. "I ain't talking to you." He took a step forward, obviously intending to scare me.

"Don't call me a bitch and get out of my room." I mimicked his voice and took a step toward him.

"I said shut up, bitch!" He snatched a fistful of my shirt and shoved me against the wall. As I reached up to shove him back, another Marine who had been waiting outside the door rushed in and grabbed my arm.

"Get out of my room, you stupid jarheads!" As soon as

149

I said it, I knew it was the wrong thing to say. Calling a Marine a jarhead is about as smart as kicking a rattlesnake in the teeth with a bare foot, but I didn't have a chance to retract my words. Kuchera finally realized that I was in trouble, but before he could move, Crawford's buddy grabbed my other arm and Crawford punched me squarely in the mouth.

Sometimes I'm amazed at my stupidity. Instead of shutting up, as Crawford had so charmingly suggested, I screamed, "I'll get you for this, Crawford! Someday you won't have anyone around to protect you and I'll wipe this floor up with your face!" Before I finished my sentence, he smashed his fist into my face again.

Most of the students in the barracks were gathered outside the door by that time, peeking around the doorway to see what all the shouting was about. As soon as Crawford hit me the second time, my hero Daniels rushed in, grabbed Crawford's shoulder, turned him around, and slugged him in the jaw. The crowd went berserk. It was just like a barroom brawl in the movies; even the women got into the action. There was a big huddle of bodies in the middle of the hallway. Occasionally an arm or a leg would shoot out of the huddle, and sometimes an entire body would slide past my doorway. They were whooping and cursing and having a grand time. I was on my way to hide in the bathroom when Kuchera ran up behind the Marine who had been holding my arms and spun him around, landing a kick in the middle of the guy's chest. Unfortunately, I was between the Marine and the wall, so Kuchera's kick sent us both sprawling. I hit the wall first and bounced back into the Marine. We both hit the wall again and I was out for the count.

When I opened my eyes, I was lying on my bed. Daniels

was leaning over me, dabbing a wad of cotton at the cut on my lip.

"Where's Crawford?" I tried to sit up, but Daniels held my shoulders.

"Crawford's gone," he said. "Hold still so I can clean those cuts. You don't want an infection." I tried to keep my mouth shut, but I couldn't.

"Is he gonna come back and kill me?" I asked, turning my head to look at the door. I bumped my lip on Daniels's hand and knocked the bloody cotton ball onto the floor. "Ouch!" I put my fingers on my lip. "That hurts!"

"It wouldn't hurt if you'd hold still," Daniels said. He pulled a fresh wad of cotton out of the bag on the desk and wet it with peroxide. "Crawford isn't gonna kill you," he said. I winced when the cotton touched my swollen lip. "Military men practice intramural fighting like college men practice football," he explained. "That's what we're trained to do and if there aren't any wars going on, we don't have much chance to practice. So, from time to time, we trade insults—anything except remarks about a guy's mother is okay—and then we smack each other around for a while, making sure we don't kill anybody. Then we shake hands and go drink a few beers."

"Aren't you glad you didn't miss the fun," I said, sarcastically. "What brought you to the barracks tonight, just in the nick of time?"

Daniels didn't answer my question. He tossed a soggy cotton ball at me. "I was crazy to worry about anybody hurting your mouth," he teased. "Crawford would have to break your jaw to get you to shut up." He flopped down in my desk chair and stretched his long, skinny legs. Usually, we talked each other's ears off, but he was being strangely silent.

"What's the matter, you cute thing you?" I fluttered my eyelashes at him, trying to get him to smile.

"Nuthin'." He aimed a most unconvincing smile at me.

"Come on!" I pleaded. "Tell me what's bothering you. Don't I always tell you?"

"It's really not anything anybody else can help me with," he explained as he sat back down. "I have to make up my mind in the next few weeks to stay in this outfit or get out," he said. "I just wanted to talk to somebody that isn't in the Army."

"Lucky for me I'm not in the Army," I said, reaching over to ruffle his hair. "You really know how to flatter a girl, don't you?"

"Shucks, you know what I mean," he blushed.

"Okay, okay," I said. "I'll be serious."

"I've had enough of Army life," Daniels said glumly. He brushed a wayward curl off his forehead. "I'll never get to go anywhere interesting as an Admin Spec, so I might as well get out and work for a company that doesn't paint everything green. I miss my family, anyway." He looked up at the poster I'd tacked to the wall. It showed a girl dressed in a boy's sailor suit, standing on the bow of a ship. The caption read: *See the World, in the U.S. Navy.* There was little chance that I'd see anything from the bow of a Navy ship, but that poster inspired me to study while everyone else was out having a good time.

"I wanted to travel in the Army," Daniels said, "but I sure didn't get far." He slumped back down into the chair.

"I know exactly what you mean," I nodded. "That's why I'm going to broadcasting school—so I can go overseas."

Daniels's face brightened and he sat up straight. "That's right! You get to pick your duty station if you get honor grades, don't you?" He was as excited as if he were the one that would be going overseas. "Do you think you'll make it this time? How are your grades?"

With only two weeks to go, I had the highest grades in class, thanks to my nightly tutoring sessions with Kuchera. Only one other student had grades as high as mine, but he was on his way through the course for a second time.

"Don't worry about Private Schmidt," Daniels said. "According to the school regs, recycles aren't allowed to be honor graduates because they've already seen all the course materials and tests."

"Are you sure?" I asked. "Chief Hatch told me Schmidt could be an honor graduate."

Daniels exhaled loudly through his nose. "Shee-it! Chief Hatch doesn't know his head from a hole in the ground. You stop by my office tomorrow and I'll give you a copy of the regulations so you can show it to him."

When I stopped by the next day to pick up the regulations, Daniels slapped me on the back. "Hey! Hey!" he said. "I see you're wearing your new stripes!" My journalist-rating badge had a spiffy white eagle and a tiny quill and scroll above a large red chevron, all embroidered on a navy-blue background. "Congratulations!" He beamed with pride.

I was feeling pretty proud of myself, too, with my new crow and my high grades, which would guarantee a genuine overseas-duty assignment. During the first week of classes, each student had filled out a "dream sheet," listing his or her first three choices of duty station. Our final grades, and the needs of the service (as interpreted by Chief Hatch), would dictate our final assignments. My first choice was the Philippines. My second and third choices were the West Coast and Hawaii. I figured that way I was certain to see palm trees, something you definitely won't find in Warren County, Pennsylvania.

Chief Hatch had called me into his office to discuss my orders. I was so excited about the prospect of my upcoming travels that I could hardly sit still as I waited for the chief to finish his standard hitch-up-the-pants, sniff 'n' sneer routine.

"Well, Johnson," he said, "I see your grades are a little better than they were the last time you were here." He enjoyed reminding me that he had helped prevent me from graduating with honors the last time I was at DINFOS.

"Well, Chief, it's hard to believe, but I see you're even fatter than you were the last time I was here," I wanted to say, but I didn't. He probably had to gain more weight periodically, so he'd have some new skin for another tattoo. As usual, whenever he talked to me, he made sure his sleeve was pushed up far enough to give me a clear view of the naked lady on his arm, so I could fully appreciate her ample endowments. The chief was such a thoughtful fella.

"Your little Army friend must be supplying you with cheat sheets," he said. I bit my lip and took a deep breath to keep from taking the bait. Chief Hatch knew I spent all my spare time studying; he was just trying to upset me. Ignoring his comments, I brushed the doughnut crumbs off the chair in front of his unkempt desk and sat down so he couldn't stare at my legs. He immediately transferred his gaze to my chest.

"This time I'm going to the Philippines," I said. Even the name sounded distant and exciting. And Chief Bagget had told me so many colorful stories about banana trees, typhoons, Negrito natives, bolo knives, and water buffalo that I could hardly wait to see them for myself.

"Sorry, Johnson." Chief Hatch picked up his coffee mug and rubbed his fingers up and down the handle, which was shaped like a nude woman. I knew he was trying to cause a reaction, so I ignored him. He took a noisy sip of coffee, then belched and snickered. "We don't have any billets for Waves in the P.I.," he said. "Besides, I got preliminary orders right here that say you're going to Cuba." He pulled a message from one of the jumbled stacks of papers on his desk.

"Cuba?" I blurted. It had to be a joke. I didn't know much about Cuba, but I knew it was a rotten duty assignment. Cuba was isolated duty. Americans were restricted to the base during the year they were assigned there.

"That's right, Johnson," the chief replied as he put down his coffee cup and picked up a candy bar wrapper and scraped up the last bit of melted chocolate with his index finger. "Are you sure you wouldn't like to give me that picture of you in a negligee?" He licked his chocolate-tipped finger and then his lips. That vulgar gesture never failed to make me lose my temper.

"You make me sick!" I jumped to my feet. "I have the highest grades in my class. That means I get to choose my orders."

He smiled. "You haven't graduated yet. Schmidt might beat you out after all."

"He can't!" I smiled triumphantly, pulling the copy of the regs out of my purse. "It says right here that he can't." I laid the paper on his desk and tapped it with my finger. The chief didn't even look at the regulations.

"Everything is subject to interpretation, Johnson," the chief insisted. "You know that." I refused to argue with him. Instead, I decided to try logic.

"They have naval stations all over the Philippines, Chief," I pointed out. "Surely there must be some Waves."

"There are, but they're all nurses," he said. "Tough titties, Johnson. Those are the breaks." Realizing that logic wouldn't work either, I sighed and picked up my books. "I see you're wearing your new stripes today," Chief Hatch said as I turned to leave. "Guess they've really lowered the standards for petty officers in the U.S. Navy, huh?"

Not interested in hearing any more insults about Waves, I walked out of his office and across the hall to the record library. Reaching up to remove a record from the top shelf, I caught a sudden movement from the corner of my eye, but before I could turn to look, something hit me in the shoulder so hard that it knocked me against a table on the other side of the room. My first thought was that Crawford had changed his mind about killing me. Holding my arm, I looked up from the floor and saw Chief Hatch looking very sheepish, standing beside the spot where I had recently been.

"Sorry, Johnson," he said, shrugging his shoulders. "I forgot you were a dame. I'm used to tacking on the men's crows and I guess I hit you a little hard."

Despite my efforts to be brave, tears were streaming down my face as I held my throbbing arm. "What did you hit me for?" I asked between sniffles.

"Don't you know about tacking on the crows?" The chief actually looked surprised.

"No."

"It's a Navy tradition," he said, squatting to bring his face level with mine. "When you get promoted to a higher pay grade, every senior enlisted person gets to punch you on the arm the first time he sees you wearing your new rating badge." He looked at my arm and frowned. "I'm used to smacking sailors. Guess I'm gonna have to hold my punches a little bit when I tack a crow on a Wave. I didn't mean to hurt you."

As he reached out to help me to my feet, I noticed that his hand was shaking and his forehead and upper lip were beaded with sweat. I didn't understand his overreaction to the situation. All he did was knock me down. Heck! My own brothers used to toss me down the stairs for recreation. Then I remembered something that Daniels had mentioned once about Chief Hatch getting in trouble for physically harassing an Army woman. He hadn't been busted, but if I reported him for hitting me, he'd be in serious trouble.

I made a horrible face. "Geez, chief! My arm really hurts." I pulled up my sleeve. I bruise very easily and my upper arm was already turning dark. "Look at this. It's black and blue. I can hardly move my arm. Maybe you dislocated my shoulder. I'd better go to the dispensary," I winced and groaned as I collected my books from under the library table where they had landed when the chief clobbered me.

"Hold on there a minute, Johnson," he said. Gently, he took my right arm and led me to a chair. "I'll get your books. Why don't you just sit down here for a minute?" I smiled at his back as he crawled under the table to retrieve a book. He struggled to his feet, out of breath, and shoved his shirttail back into his waistband. "Why don't you just take the rest of the afternoon off?" he wheezed. "I'll cover you with your instructors. Just get some ice and go lay down and rest that arm." The library was air-conditioned, but Chief Hatch was sweating.

"Okay, Chief," I said, my voice filled with as much pain as I could muster.

The next morning, I was in Chief Hatch's office bright and early. "Look at this!" I rolled up my sleeve to reveal a bruise that stretched from my shoulder to my elbow. "Pretty colorful, don't you think?" I asked. My entire upper arm was green, with dark purple and blue spots.

For once, Chief Hatch didn't have a snappy comeback.

Without a word, he pulled out a cigarette and lit it, all the while staring at my arm.

"Don't you think I'd better go to the dispensary and get it checked out?" I asked. "Wonder what they'll say when they find out that a chief petty officer hit me. They don't go around punching women in the Army when they get promoted, you know. They shake their hands. They sure do have some strange traditions, don't they?"

Chief Hatch laid his cigarette down so the burning end hung over the edge of his desk and hurried around to pull out a chair for me. I knew he had to be desperate to resort to gallantry.

"Look, Johnson, why don't you sit down a minute," he said. "I was just about to make a phone call that might interest you. The journalist detailer is an old friend of mine and he might be able to swing a billet for you in the P.I." He snapped his fingers. "Damn! I was gonna wait until I got that picture of you before I called him, but maybe I'll do it out of the goodness of my heart."

"Why don't you do that, Chief?" I said, wishing I could smack him in the face, just once.

A few minutes later, he hung up and smacked the top of his desk with his palms. "Okay, Johnson," he said, lighting another cigarette and slowly inhaling. "I got authorization for you. You got orders to Clark Air Base, Republic of the Philippines. It's an Air Force base, but we got Navy personnel at the American Forces Philippines Network." He exhaled into the air instead of in my face, as he usually did.

"Thanks, Chief," I said, flashing a dazzling smile at his grumpy face. "I'll send you a postcard."

"You'll get along fine over there in the P.I.," Chief Hatch said as he flicked the ash off his cigarette onto the floor. "They don't stick price tags on stuff. You just pick what you like and then bargain for it." He shook his head. "You'll bankrupt the poor suckers."

12

Mabuhay

"Ya-hoo!" Daniels cheered and scooped me up off the ground when I told him the good news about my orders. "I wish I could have been there to see Chief Hatch's face." Hugging me tight, he spun me around on the sidewalk in front of his barracks, slipped on an icy spot, and dumped us both into a snow drift. Automatically, I lay down on my back and swept my arms up and down, making indentations in the snow.

"What the heck are you doing?" Daniels propped himself up on his elbows and stared at me.

"Haven't you ever seen anyone make a snow angel before?" I wrinkled my nose at him. "We used to do it all the time when I was a kid."

"No," Daniels said, shaking his head.

I jumped up and pushed him down onto his back. "Then you were deprived of one of the great delights of childhood and it's my duty as an American citizen to correct that deficiency. Flap your arms up and down," I instructed, as I yanked on his arms.

"Wait! Wait!" he shouted. "I almost forgot!" He reached into his pocket and pulled out a small blue book. "Here's something I got for you, to celebrate your orders to the P.I. I've been saving it for a surprise."

I glanced at the cover of the book. *Speak Tagalog in Ten Easy Lessons.* "This is great! Just what I need." I

159

jumped down next to him and gave him another quick hug. "Come on," I said, pulling him to his feet. "Walk me to the barracks before we get arrested for making unauthorized public displays of affection while in uniform." I linked my elbow through his and gave him a tug in the direction of the parade ground that separated the two barracks.

I opened the phrase book and began reading as we crunched across the frozen field. Daniels put his arm around my shoulder and pulled me toward him. "I sure do hate to see you go," he said. "Guess I'm kind of attached to you."

"I'm crazy about you, too," I said, still reading. "But I'll have to force myself to travel to a gorgeous tropical island and slave away behind a hot TV camera to protect the freedom of the press, democracy, and the American way." I sighed. "Sometimes a woman just has to do what a woman has to do."

Daniels squeezed my arm. "Shoot, I wouldn't ask you to give up your orders," he said. "Even Chief Hatch couldn't get away with that!" He leaned down and rested the top of his chin on my head. "But you're gonna be a long ways from home. Aren't you afraid you'll get lonely?"

"Yeah." I pointed to a phrase. "Guess I'd better learn this one—*Gusto ka bang magsayaw?* It means 'Do you want to dance?'"

"You could do that. Or you could take somebody to the P.I. with you," Daniels said.

"Sure," I laughed. "I could get married and take along my husband as a military dependent. Ha! That would be a quick way to end a romance, wouldn't it?" Daniels slowed his pace as we reach the steps of my barracks. I started to walk up, but he pulled on my arm, stopping me halfway.

"I think it would be okay, *if* you married the right man," he said. Something in his voice made me forget about the phrase book and look at him. He was standing a couple of steps below me, dancing from one foot to the other. He looked up at me for a second and then looked at his feet, as though surprised to find they were connected to the rest of his body. He cleared his throat and brushed some imaginary hair off his forehead. "I'll be out of the Army pretty soon, you know," he said to his feet.

"Yeah?" I said, hesitantly. It had finally dawned on me that Daniels might be leading up to something.

"If we got married, I could go with you." He spoke so quickly and quietly that I wasn't sure I'd heard him correctly.

"Married!" I squeaked.

"Why not?" He reached up and closed my mouth, which was hanging open. "It happens all the time. Nothing to be ashamed of. Some of the best families have married people in them."

"Married," I repeated. I bit my lip and closed my eyes, trying to imagine myself as a married person. A vivid picture popped into my head of a small house on a narrow street, with a broken tricycle lying on its side in the unmowed front lawn, and three grimy-faced little tykes squabbling over a deflated beach ball. I rubbed my eyes and tried to create an image of newly-wedded bliss.

"Aw, for Chrissake!" Daniels cussed and smacked the railing beside the steps. "If the idea of marrying me gives you such a headache, just forget it," he said. "I was only joking, anyway." He backed away. "Look, I have some things to take care of tonight. I'll see you around." He took off down the street.

"Daniels!" I yelled, but he didn't slow down. I plopped down on the steps, trying to decide what to do. Daniels was even more stubborn than I was, and I knew his pride wouldn't let him come back and talk to me. He'd wait for me to make the next move and I didn't know what that would be. Now that I finally had a chance to travel, after all that work, I had to meet a real special man. If I was back home in Youngsville, I'd have married him in a heartbeat. But I couldn't get married and go to the P.I., that was for sure. Daniels would hate being a military dependent, no matter how hard he tried. But he'd never believe I refused to marry him out of consideration for his happiness. I sure wouldn't believe some guy if he said he loved me but wouldn't marry me because he wanted me to be happy.

"Are you sick?" I hadn't heard the private on duty at the barracks come outside and stand beside me. "You've been sitting out here a long time, rubbing the back of your neck and shaking your head," she said.

"I'm all right." I stood up. "I was just thinking." I walked up the steps, collected my mail, and headed towards my room.

"Hey!" the private called. "Don't forget this." She picked up the Tagalog phrase book, which I'd dropped on the steps, and flipped through it. "This looks interesting. You going to the Philippines?" she asked.

"Yes, I am."

"Lucky for you." She handed me the book.

"Yeah," I nodded. "I'm pretty lucky."

Dear Ingrate,

I should have known that you'd be too dumb to appreciate all the trouble I went through just to make sure you had somebody to play with. I knew you'd sit around and mope and spend all your time doing homework instead of having fun, if I didn't lend you a hand. But I guess it didn't do any good, though, if you're still trying to be an honor graduate. I don't know why you insist on compet-

ing with men—it just pisses them off. Sometime, you should find a guy you don't have to compete with for a change and just like him. But you never listen to anybody's advice and you can't resist a challenge, can you? I guess you have something to prove to somebody. Maybe this time you'll succeed and then you can relax and enjoy life a little.

You should have been here last month. You're the one who's always looking for excitement and adventure. We had a real live racial incident at the barracks. You remember Barb and Bonnie Clarke (the sisters from Omaha), don't you? Well, Bonnie was secretly dating this black guy and Liz Brown (the girl with the big Afro who works in Personnel) found out and got real pissed. Apparently, all Caucasians look alike to Liz, because she jumped Barb in the laundry room and started smacking her around, telling her to stop hanging out with brothers. Barb didn't know what was going on, because Bonnie never told her about this guy. Anyway, Liz and Barb both got busted and had to go to Captain's Mast. Liz went over to the dispensary and got one of her friends to make her up a cast for her ankle and she limped around, telling everybody that Barb kicked her. Barb never did know what was going on—you know she never thinks about anything but that lying sailor Freddy, who's been promising to come and marry her for the past three years.

Anyway, Barb ended up getting busted because she's a second-class petty officer and she got in a fight, even though she didn't start it. The CO said she shouldn't have allowed herself to get in that position. Liz just got put on probation. Everybody's pissed. They think Liz got off easy because she's black, which is probably true.

That's not the end of the story, though. Barb was at the end of her enlistment when she got busted, so instead of reupping to hang around and pine for Freddy for another four years, she said the hell with the Navy and Freddy and went back home to Nebraska. A couple of weeks after she left, good old Freddy showed up with a diamond ring and found out Barb was gone, so he bought an old clunker and took off for Nebraska. His car broke down and he got caught in a blizzard, but he finally made it to Nebraska—the day after Barb married her high-school sweetheart. Can you believe it? I never saw so many unlucky things happen to one girl in my whole life. If I saw it in a movie, I'd think they made it up because it's too sad. But that's not the worst part. Bonnie ended up getting pregnant, so they kicked her out of the Navy. Now they're both back in Nebraska. I betcha the recruiter in their home town is gonna have a heck of a time enlisting any women for a while.

I sure hope I have better luck with men than the Clarke sisters did. Now, don't go jumping to any conclusions, but I've been dating this sailor named Tony Randinelli from Connecticut. He came up to me in the hallway at work one day and said, "Excuse me. Could you tell me where I could get a drink of water?" I could tell he was from my neck of the Northeast because he pronounced water the right way, like 'watah,' so I personally escorted him to the nearest drinking fountain. Anyway, he told me I was charming and good-looking and asked me out to dinner. Since he's obviously intelligent and has excellent taste in women, I figured, what the heck, I'll do him a favor and go out with him.

That's all the news from Norfolk. Take it easy. I'm going home for three weeks at Christmas, so you'll be out of school by the time I get back. Send me a postcard from the P.I., you lifer.

Mabuhay,*
Your Pal
*It means "to your health" in Tagalog, you peabrain!

This wouldn't be the first time I spent the holidays away from home. At Norfolk, I had Christmas duty my first year on board. When I complained to Chief Bagget, he said, "The national defense doesn't take Christmas vacation. Somebody always has to be on duty. You'll get used to it.

164

After a few years in the service, Christmas is just another day."

The cooks at the chow hall prepared a big turkey dinner with cranberries, sweet potatoes, and pumpkin pie, but there was something depressing about eating Christmas dinner from a gray tray at a long Formica-topped table with forty or fifty unrelated people, even if there were poinsettia centerpieces on the table and frosted reindeers on the windows.

This year, Daniels and I had talked about going to downtown Indianapolis for dinner, but I figured he had probably changed his mind after our disastrous discussion about marriage.

I took a hot shower and went to bed early, hoping to fall asleep and not have to think about anything, but I tossed and turned until after midnight. I got up and turned on my desk lamp, opened the bottom drawer, and pulled out my box of letters from home. I'd been saving them since boot camp, so I had over a hundred. They were filled with photographs and details of my family's life—my brother grinning self-consciously behind a bowling trophy, Mom showing off her slimmer figure, my cousin's wedding, my sister's new baby, a stray dog that adopted my dad, Grandma's birthday cake with eighty candles. Sitting at my desk, surrounded by my letters, I felt like Stella Dallas in that old movie where she stands outside in the rain, looking into the window of a warmly lighted house to watch her daughter's wedding.

"You sure are cute, even if you are the most pigheaded female I ever did see," Daniels leaned over my shoulder and whispered in my ear. My mouth was full of scrambled eggs, so I raised my eyebrows at him. "You thought I was mad at you, right?" he asked. I nodded, still chewing.

165

"Well, I been thinking about our conversation," he said, as he sat down and slapped a tablespoon of butter on his grits. I hurried to swallow my eggs.

"I've been thinking, too," I nodded.

"Don't tell me." He held up his fork. "Let me guess."

"Okay."

Daniels was either nervous or in a hurry. He stuffed a forkful of grits into his mouth and kept on talking. "You love me, but you can't marry me and take me to the P.I. as your dependent because you know that I'm a good old southern boy at heart—despite my modern, liberal philosophy—and it would make me crazier than a coot to be beholden to a woman for my bed and board."

"But—"

"Wait!" he said. "Let me finish." I nodded and he continued. "If you stayed with me because you love me, and didn't go to the Philippines—I know you have to go, I'm just supposing—you'd resent me forever for depriving you of your adventure. Even if I am the most lovable man you ever met." He finished his grits and his speech in the same bite and sat back with a satisfied smile. "Well, am I right?"

"Shucks," I drawled. "I reckon you done figured out the whole dang thang."

He flicked my rating badge with his finger. "Have some respect for your military superiors, would you?" he said. He drank half his glass of milk in one swallow, wiped his mouth with the back of his hand, and cleared his throat. "Well, then, it's settled. We'll be sweet-talking pen pals until you come back home. Then we'll just see what happens. Okay with you?"

Daniels was a terrible liar. He was obviously pretending that I hadn't hurt his feelings. That meant that he really did love me, which made it even harder for me to hurt his feelings. But he was right. He wasn't a man who would enjoy having an independent wife. He needed someone who would depend on him.

"Okay with me," I agreed. He looked at his watch and stood up.

"Gotta run," he said and drained his glass of milk. "See you at your graduation tomorrow, Miss Honor Graduate."

"You forgot to read the small print, Johnson." The chief shoved a piece of paper under my nose. "It says right here 'at the discretion of the Commanding Officer.'" He was holding the copy of the regulations that prohibited recycled students from graduating with honors.

The grades hadn't been posted yet, but Chief Hatch, anxious to pay me back for making him change my orders, had called me to his office. He couldn't wait to give me the news so he could gloat. Schmidt was going to be designated the honor graduate for the class, with higher grades than mine by one-tenth of a point.

"Of course, the CO asked the senior enlisted Navy man on board for a recommendation," Chief Hatch said. He paused to inhale, forcing his stomach to masquerade as a chest for a few seconds. "I told him you were a good student, but I had to tell him that Schmidt is an out-damn-standing soldier."

There was no point in arguing with the chief; he always managed to win, because he had no respect for anyone, including himself. My orders were official. I'd soon be on my way overseas—that wouldn't change. But I had really counted on being the honor graduate. I had worked so hard and I just couldn't believe that an overgrown schoolyard bully could rob me of my due reward with just a few words whispered in the proper ear. I stared at Chief Hatch, too stunned to react. He sat down and leaned back in his chair, stretched his arms in the air, and then clasped his hands behind his head.

"You must really hate me, Chief," I said softly, "to sink so low. You even helped the Army beat the Navy, just to hurt me."

"I don't hate you, Johnson," he said as he rubbed his belly. "But you broads don't have any business in this man's Navy. It's as simple as that."

"Simple is a good word to describe that man!" I crumpled the grade report Chief Hatch had given me and threw it on my desk. Then I threw myself down on my bunk. "All that work for nothing!" I looked at the stack of notebooks I'd spent the past six weeks studying day and night. "Ooh! I wish this was his fat head!" I hammered my pillow with both fists.

"Lucas was right!" I muttered. "I never should have come back to this crummy school." I picked up my scissors and chopped the report to pieces. That felt so good that I hacked one of my assignment books to bits. By the time all my notebooks were destroyed, I was asleep at my desk.

I almost didn't go to the graduation ceremony, but I refused to give Chief Hatch the satisfaction of knowing that he'd succeeded in making me miserable, so I put on my spiffiest uniform and my most gracious smile. Before the official rigamarole started, more than one of my classmates whispered in my ear that they thought I got a shitty deal. "Oh, what's the difference if I get a pen and pencil set or a laminated plaque?" I answered them with a haughty wave of my limp wrist. Nobody congratulated Private Schmidt, who stood off in the corner by himself.

"I would have rather had the plaque," Schmidt whispered after the CO's job-well-done speech, as we stood in front of the class, waiting for the applause to die down so we could take our seats. "Your award is a lot nicer than mine." I knew he was trying to make me feel better, but I wasn't in the mood to be mollified.

"Well, you could have offered to take this stupid plaque," I snapped.

"I did, but they wouldn't let me," he said. "Chief Hatch told me if I made a stink, he'd see to it that I got recycled again." Schmidt looked so sad that I couldn't help feeling sorry for him. Everyone was mad at him, and it wasn't his fault. All he did was study harder the second time around and get good grades. He wasn't responsible for the last-minute change in the rules.

"No hard feelings, Schmidt." I stuck out my hand. "Good luck in your new assignment."

He grasped my hand and shook it with fervor. "You're a good sport, Johnson," he said. "I admire that."

"Right," I agreed. "Too bad there's no award for Best Sport."

Kuchera took my hand as soon as I convinced Schmidt to let go of it. "Thanks, Johnson," Kuchera said. "If it wasn't for you, I probably wouldn't have made it." He looked at his diploma and stood up a little straighter, smiling to himself.

"You helped me too, you know," I told him.

"Me?" he snorted. "I didn't help you. If it wasn't for me, Crawford wouldn't have gave you a bloody lip."

"Hey, don't worry about that," I said. "I needed a little defensive combat training anyway."

Being a good sport was making me tired, so I looked around for Daniels. We had agreed that he wouldn't take me to the airport because we'd both cry and get depressed, but we thought we could handle a walk to the barracks without any major emotional breakdowns.

Chief Hatch stood in the back of the room, near the door, with the other instructors; I could feel him watching me, but I didn't even acknowledge his presence enough to ignore him. Instead, I looked right through him as I took Daniels's arm and strolled out the door. I paused on the threshold just long enough to drop the plaque into the trash can. It made a satisfying clang.

Daniels and I talked about everything except us on the way to the barracks. I knew as well as he did that he'd go back home and miss me for a while before he married some cute little country girl who'd look up to him and depend on him, but we both pretended that we really believed we'd see each other again.

"You be sure to write, now, you hear?" he said. Conscious of the fact that we were wearing our uniforms and surrounded by people, we quickly kissed. I swallowed hard and walked into the barracks without looking back. After checking my locker to make sure I hadn't left anything behind, I slung my purse over my shoulder, grabbed a suitcase in each hand, and headed out the main gate of Fort Ben. I could see the classroom building through the grimy window of the bus shelter. "This time," I whispered. "I swear I'm never coming back here again—dead or alive."

As soon as I boarded the bus, I pulled the manila envelope containing my orders out of my purse to read those beautiful words one more time.

Journalist Third-Class LouAnne Johnson, U.S.N., is hereby ordered to report to the Officer of the Day, Clark Air Base, Republic of the Philippines, on or before 0001 on 28 January, 1972, for assignment to the American Forces Philippines Network.

Hugging the papers to my chest, I closed my eyes, leaned back in the seat, and hummed as I indulged myself in my favorite daydream. Disembarking from a small prop jet, I'd pause in the doorway to shade my eyes with my white-gloved hand, searching for my family, who would nudge one another and say, "Hey, look, there's LouAnne! Doesn't she look sharp in that uniform with the fancy insignia on her sleeve?" and "Hurry, Pa! Get a picture of her coming down the steps."

After a week of hugging grandmothers, eating homemade apple pies, admiring the new teeth of my vaguely familiar nieces and nephews, and amusing my brothers and sisters with amazing-but-true sea stories, I'd pack up my gear, sling my seabag over my shoulder, kiss my mother, shake my father's hand, and wave to my envious siblings as I headed up the steps of another plane, enroute for California—final destination, the Philippines.

13

Hold the
Balut, Please

Even Grandpa Carl Oscar "Pickle Puss" Johnson, who
doesn't trust airplanes any more than he does indoor
plumbing or men who wear pink shirts, went to the airport
to see me off. There was a short delay before takeoff as the
ground crew chased two white-tailed deer off the end of the
runway. I pressed my face against the window for one last
glimpse of my family, standing amid the ten-foot snow-
drifts outside the small building that housed the entire
airport of Bradford, Pennsylvania. Despite the sub-zero
temperatures and gusty winds, my parents, grandparents,
two brothers, and two sisters smiled and waved and blew
me kisses that instantly turned into little puffs of steam.

Thirty hours and three airplanes later, I pressed my
nose against the window and peered at the Philippine jungle as we circled Clark Air Base. The colors were too vivid
to be real. Vegetation so thick it looked like bright green
fur covered the mountainsides and the sky was that peculiar too-perfect postcard blue. After two frostbitten weeks
home on leave, I could hardly wait to feel the tropical
sunshine.

When I stepped out of the military transport jet, the air
smacked me in the face like a damp, hot towel and the
sunlight made my eyes water so much that I could barely
see the air terminal through the heat waves that shim-

mered above the blacktopped runway. I closed my eyes and took a deep breath. Even the air smelled different, a mixture of perspiration, tropical flowers, and diesel exhaust.

Anxious to get my first taste of the genuine native lifestyle, I had arrived a day early so I could spend my first night in a hotel off base instead of checking into the barracks. After I passed through customs, an Air Force sergeant handed me a statement to sign that said I wasn't bringing any birth-control devices, including birth-control pills, into the country.

"I wonder why they care if some woman takes the pill," I spoke to myself, but the sailor standing in line behind me answered.

"They don't want you American women bringing any of your evil, liberal philosophies over here to contaminate the innocent Filipinas," he said.

"You're probably right." I smiled, assuming the man was making a joke.

He noticed my grin. "I'm serious," he said. "The women here are *real* women—nothing like Stateside females." He sighed and put one hand over his heart, as though he were pledging the flag. "Filipinas cook delicious food, clean the house, wash the clothes by hand, have babies, and follow orders. Real women. I'm gonna retire and stay here forever."

He picked up his bag and headed out the door before I could offer my thanks on behalf of the Stateside female population for his plan to deprive us of a man with such excruciatingly excellent taste. I signed the form promising not to prevent the birth of any Filipino children, collected my seabag, and walked out of the main gate into another world.

A one-lane dirt road led through the center of the little

173

village of Balibago. Miniature black-haired people filled the streets, and everyone had a bundle under one arm—net bags filled with fresh vegetables, tiny golden-brown babies, live chickens. The men wore loose cotton pants and light-colored shirts. The young women wore bright colorful skirts and blouses, but the older women wore sari-like dresses made from single pieces of cloth draped over their shoulders. The dresses covered them from neck to ankles, but they looked much cooler than I felt in my lightweight blue uniform. I was the only person on the street wearing shoes. Everyone else wore sandals or nothing on their feet.

People stared at me as I walked down the street, peering into the stores filled with wooden carvings, capiz-shell lamps, and wicker furniture. At first, I was flattered by the attention, but after a couple of hours, I felt like screaming, "Look at somebody else for a minute, will you?"

I ducked into a shop, hoping to find a few minutes of privacy. A small boy squatted in front of a high-back throne chair. His fingers moved with rapid precision as he wove an intricate pattern of wicker across the back of the chair. He paused and asked, "You like buy, lady?"

"How much?" I said.

"Two hundred peso," he said.

"Two hundred!" I said, automatically thinking in dollars.

"One hundred peso," he said. "Fourteen dollar."

"Fourteen dollars for a chair!" I exclaimed. "That's ridiculous!" I thought the price was ridiculously low for such a gorgeous piece of furniture, but he thought I meant the price was too high.

"Eighty peso?" he offered.

"I'll be back when I need some furniture," I told him.

"Seventy-five peso?" he called as I left the store.

On the street, traffic moved slowly, maneuvering around the children, chickens, bicycles, buses, and psychedelic jeepneys. The jeeps were painted like circus wagons, with streamers, fringed windows, and elaborate chrome hood ornaments. Someone would wave a hand, make a kissing noise. The jeepney would slow down and the new passenger would jump into the back and ride a few blocks, then hop out and toss the driver a coin.

I stopped on the corner to watch a young man run alongside a bus, handing cigarettes to the passengers. Then he pulled out a matchbook and ran in the other direction, lighting the cigarettes in a row.

Boys and girls walked amid the moving traffic, offering sticks of chewing gum, magazines, newspapers, cigarettes, and candy to the travelers. Old men carried large bags of steaming corn on the cob, yelling, *"Maiz! Maiz!"*

A stooped old man with baby-smooth skin approached, holding out a bag containing what looked like eggs with mud and grass caked on the outside. *"Balut! Balut!"* he called. He stopped in front of me and dangled the dirty eggs in front of my face. I shrugged my shoulders and held up my palms. He took an egg, held it above his mouth, and cracked it. A partially formed baby bird, complete with beak and feet, dripped out of the shell and down his throat, leaving behind a pungent, peculiar odor. The old man swallowed and rubbed his stomach. *"Balut?"* He jiggled the bag.

"No." I gagged and waved him away. He shook his head in pity for someone unable to appreciate such a true delicacy and shuffled off in pursuit of customers with more cosmopolitan palates. He had only traveled a few feet, when I ran to catch up with him. I tapped him on the shoulder and held up six fingers. He gave me a half-dozen smelly eggs and a toothless grin.

"Masarap." He nodded. "You like." I had no intention of eating the eggs to find out what *masarap* meant. I

planned to buy some shellac and cover them so they wouldn't stink, paint them, and send them to Lucas as an Easter gift, telling her that they were a specialty of the Philippines and she must promise to peel at least one, even though they were hand painted just for her. She'd get a big surprise when she cracked that egg, all right, and she'd think twice before she mailed any more love letters with my signature on them to Army sergeants.

As soon as I took out my wallet to pay for the eggs, I was surrounded by barefoot raggedy children. They held out their grimy little hands and looked at me with big eyes. "Peso? Centavo?" they pleaded. "Hungry, hungry." I couldn't ignore them, so I handed out all my change. The more I handed out, the more kids appeared. Finally, I put my wallet away, but the children followed me, tugging on my sleeves, begging me to let them carry my sea bag for a few pennies. I thought then that I knew how movie stars feel, trying to walk down the street like normal people, but after a short while, the attention began to make my skin prickle. Just as I was starting to panic, I saw a hotel across the street. I made a mad dash between a purple-and-orange jeep and two bicycles.

The bellboy, looking like a little kid in his big brother's Boy Scout uniform, took my bag and chased the children away. "Sssst!" he hissed and waved his hand. The children giggled and ran off. The bellboy shook his head and addressed me in English. "Children not starving. They buy candy and tell everyone how you look. Next time you outside, whole town follow you."

"Wonderful," I said, delighted to find someone speaking English. "Do you have a room?"

"Special deluxe room." He grinned up at me. I followed him through a courtyard filled with glorious fragrant flowers to a small room with a single bed, a cheap orange vinyl-covered chair, and a sink. He turned on the water in the sink, crossed his arms, and stood back, looking at me. He obviously expected some kind of reaction, so I took a closer look at the sink. I thought maybe it was carved from water buffalo teeth or something, but it was made out of standard white sink material. Noting my confusion, the bellboy hurried into the bathroom and turned on the shower with a flourish. Running water seemed to be a scientific wonder that I should appreciate—and I certainly did. It was over one hundred degrees outside and not much cooler inside. I cupped my hands, filled them with water, and started to drink.

"*Hinde!*" he shouted, turning off the water.

"*Hinde?*" I repeated. He smiled, blinding me with a flash of white teeth against his brown face, held up a finger, and ran from the room. In a second, he returned with two lukewarm bottles of beer. He opened one, poured it into a glass, and offered it to me with a little bow. As a general rule, I hate beer, but I was too thirsty to be picky.

"*Masarap?*" the bellboy asked, patting his stomach.

"*Masarap,*" I said, hoping I hadn't asked for a rotten egg. Apparently, I hadn't. He gave me a little salute and walked to the door, where he paused. Some things are universal—bellboys always wait for tips. I pulled out a dollar bill and handed it to him.

"*Salamat po!* Thank you!" he said, bobbing his head and grinning. "Thank you berry much. Thank you. *Maraming salamat.*" His overwhelming gratitude puzzled me for a few minutes, until I realized that, because of the currency exchange rate, I had given him an eight-dollar tip. Not bad for turning on the water and bringing me a warm beer.

As soon as he closed the door, I peeled off my sticky clothes and headed for the bathroom. I planned to have a cool shower and a relaxing stroll in the sunset before dinner. When I turned on the hot water spigot, a roach the size of a Chihuahua shot out of the shower spout. He waved his antlers at me, then ran up the wall and out the window. I stepped backward and abruptly sat down on the toilet. Immediately, something slimy squeezed between my toes and ran up my leg. I screeched and jumped up as a small lizard fell off my leg and skittered out of the bathroom. Two more roaches crawled out from under the toilet seat and stood waving at me.

In a single leap, I cleared the ten feet separating me from the bed. Tearing the covers open, I wrapped a sheet around me and sat gasping and shaking in the middle of the mattress. There are plenty of bugs and creepy creatures out in the country where I grew up, but they didn't take showers with me or keep me company on the toilet. My whole body felt prickly, like bugs were crawling all over me. My appetite was gone, along with my desire to explore my new surroundings. I decided to skip dinner and get a good night's sleep. I checked to make sure there weren't any new creatures on the bed behind me and flopped down on my back. One look at the ceiling and I froze. It was covered with tiny flesh-colored lizards, darting back and forth, catching bugs with practiced skill. I watched them with horror until I realized that they weren't big enough to eat me, even if they were interested. Besides, there were enough bugs on that ceiling to feed them for weeks.

Exhausted, I nearly drifted off to sleep, but I made the mistake of turning my head on the pillow as a roach crawled up over the side of the bed. He retreated when I beat on the mattress, but I knew he was under the bed waiting for me. The beer made me have to use the bathroom, but I was afraid to go. I didn't want to put my feet on the floor, in case some other slithery thing was living under the bed, but when my teeth started to float, I tiptoed to the bathroom, still wearing my sheet. I stood in the doorway for a while, then ever-so-quietly approached the toilet. The second I sat down, the roach appeared, along with his buddies. They scurried around the bathroom, laughing at me as I ran back to the bed, the sheet flapping around my knees.

I waited for a few minutes, then jumped out of bed, rushed to the bathroom, and was back again in less than thirty seconds. That's how long it took for the vigilante roach squad to round up the volunteers to come and have a few chuckles by scaring the new girl in town.

The rest of the night I spent sitting in the middle of the bed, fending off the roaches. I was in pretty sad shape when I checked into work the next day, but the commanding officer didn't seem to notice the circles under my eyes. Commander Willenbrau shook my hand and gave me my first assignment—as the weather lady on the live TV and radio newscasts each night. I was thrilled. My first day onboard and already I was going to be an official announcer on AFPN, the American Forces Philippines Network.

The CO introduced me to the staff; as usual, I was the only woman and the junior person in the group, which consisted of six Navy men, four Air Force sergeants, and two Marines. A tall, skinny second-class Navy petty officer named Jeff Ball was assigned as my sponsor. In addition to teaching me my job at the station, Ball would help me learn my way around the base and give me pointers about native customs. He was married to a Filipina and lived off base in the barrio, so he was considered the resident expert on intercultural relations. Although his name was Jeff, everyone called him Jep, because that's how his wife pronounced his name. Some of the guys at work heard her call him Jep and the name stuck. Jep told me that the Tagalog alphabet doesn't have an *f* in it, so the natives often mix up words with *f*s and *p*s.

"Don't be surprised if someone invites you to a farty," he said. "Just ask them if you should bring some pood."

The leading petty officer was a hefty first-class journalist named Al Stratter who was trying to quit smoking and constantly chewed red plastic swizzle sticks. Stratter didn't appear to be overjoyed at the thought of having a woman on board. He looked me up and down and rearranged his private parts.

"Well, I guess it's okay as long as you stick to fluff stuff, like the weather," he said around his stick. "You ready to start tonight?"

"Tonight?" I glanced at my watch. It was already four o'clock, or 1600 hours in nautical lingo.

"What's the matter?" Stratter asked. "You're a broadcaster, aren't you? Or do you need special training because you're a girl?"

I squared my shoulders. "I'm ready," I said.

"Okay." Stratter spat out his mangled chewing stick and immediately replaced it with a new one. "Be on the set at 1700 hours. You're on the air, live, at 1800."

I spent the next hour practicing the weather forecast in the empty studio. The local forecast for our island, Luzon, wasn't hard to memorize. Since it was the dry season, the entire forecast consisted of, "It was hot today, it was hot yesterday, and it'll be hot tomorrow." When the rainy season started, the weather report changed to, "It rained today, it rained yesterday, and it will rain tomorrow." No wonder Stratter didn't think I needed to practice. Even a girl could handle that kind of forecast.

After the local weather, I had to slide the map of Luzon

over to reveal the U.S. map, point out the high and low temperatures in the States, and describe the various storms and fronts moving across the country. Service people got a big kick out of knowing when it rained or snowed on the folks back home.

Stratter was the first crew member to arrive for the evening broadcast. He acknowledged my presence with a flip of his swizzle stick and assigned the rest of the crew to their positions as switcher, director, and audio, film chain, and camera operators. He took his place behind camera #1 and told me to stand by for his cue.

I whispered the forecast over and over to myself as the other announcers gave the news and sportscasts. After a break for a public service announcement, the red light came on and Stratter cued me. I smiled into the camera and said, "Good evening, ladies and gentlemen, let's take a look at the local weather," as Stratter dropped his drawers, turned around, and mooned me. I blushed and dropped the wooden pointer, picked it up, and knocked the microphone off my collar.

Fortunately, Jep was directing. He switched to a sixty-second spot and I had a minute to recuperate before the camera pointed my way again. As soon as the newscast was over, I ran behind the set, determined not to cry in front of the crew. I knew that the CO had been watching the big monitor in his office. He'd probably fire me. I'd have the shortest career in the history of AFPN—one whole day as an official broadcaster. Jep heard me sniffling and walked behind the weather maps.

"Hey, don't get upset. It was just a joke," Jep said. "Big Al always does that to initiate a new broadcaster into the group. He wanted to see if you could handle an emergency on air." He laughed and patted my arm. "You did pretty good, except for turning so red. The engineers adjusted the color, so the audience probably didn't even notice the difference."

"I was terrible," I sniffed.

"Yeah," Jep admitted. "But Big Al does that to every new announcer, so the CO never expects much the first time. Big Al will behave himself next time and you'll do fine. Then he'll tell the CO that he gave you a few pointers and the CO will be impressed with his leadership ability."

I collapsed against the wall. "It is kind of funny," I admitted. "If I wasn't so tired, I probably would have laughed."

"How come you're so tired?" Jep asked. "You've only been here one day. It's probably the heat."

"Either that or the roaches and lizards," I said. I told him about spending the night fending them off.

"The geckos, that's the name of the lizards, are okay," Jep said. "They only eat bugs. Kind of like mosquito control. But the roaches are pretty bad, unless you keep your house really clean." He puffed out his bony chest. "You should see my house. My wife and the housegirl wash our floor every day. It's so clean it squeaks when you walk in your bare feet." His pride was so obvious and sincere that I had to smile.

"That's better," he said. "Hey! Why don't you come over for dinner? Your barracks is nothing to rush home to. Besides, my wife would be thrilled. She loves American women. She thinks they're all beautiful." I followed him out from behind the set.

"I'd love to come to your house for dinner, Jep," I said, "but I'm supposed to check into the barracks tonight. I don't want to get in trouble."

"You won't get in trouble." Jep picked up a camera cable and deftly coiled it around his arm. "Welcome to overseas shore duty. If you do your job, you don't have to worry too much about rules and regulations."

182

He walked around the set, putting things away, making sure the cameras had the lens caps in place. "I'll just check the light box and then we'll go have some dinner," he said.

"Shouldn't you call and let your wife know you're bringing someone?" I asked.

"Ha!" Jep laughed. "People off base don't have phones," he said. "There's a two-year waiting list to get a phone, and even if you have one, you can't get a good connection for more than five miles. There's no one to call, anyway. Only the rich Filipinos have phones." He piled the cables in circles and pushed the TV cameras against the wall. "Don't worry," he said. "We feed so many people, one more mouth won't matter." As it turned out, he meant the statement literally.

Three barefoot girls with gleaming black hair that flowed down their backs to their knees ran out of the house to meet the car as we pulled into the driveway. I thought they were all children, but Jep introduced the tallest one —the top of her head almost reached my shoulder—as his wife, Luz. She gave me a shy smile, took my hand, and led me into the house. The housegirl, Lydia, wasn't much bigger than my seabag, but she insisted on carrying it for me. Marites, the maid, followed silently behind us. Inside the pink stucco house, an old woman stood holding a perfectly beautiful baby with huge dark eyes and tiny pink pierced earrings.

"This Lola," Luz said, then spoke to the woman in Tagalog. "She my mother." Lola smiled at me. Her hands were gnarled and wrinkled, but her face was as smooth as the face of the infant in her arms. Luz took the gurgling baby. "And this Marabel," she said.

The women all stared at me as we sat around the table, but the food was so scrumptious that I wasn't bothered as much as I'd been when people stared at me on the street. Their staring was interrupted every few minutes by a knock on the door. Half the neighborhood stopped by for dinner. Marites or Lydia would wrap some rice, vegetables, and barbecued meat in a banana leaf and hand it out the door. I didn't say anything, but Jep noticed my confusion.

"They're all relatives of my wife," he said, nodding towards the door. "We feed a lot of people on my paycheck, but it's part of the package." Luz stretched up to kiss his cheek. Ball put his arm around her and smiled at me. "And the package is well worth it."

"If I were a relative, I'd come by for dinner, even if I had money," I said. "This dish is wonderful. What is it?"

Luz blushed, flattered by the compliment. "Pork *adobo,*" she said, pointing to a bowl of sautéed meat. "Very easy." She touched a bowl of thin, transparent noodles sprinkled with chunks of vegetables and meat. "This *pancit.*" She put another crisp egg roll on my plate. "*Lumpia Shanghai* not so easy."

Jep disappeared to take a nap while Luz explained how to make the various dishes. I started to help Lydia and Marites clear the table, but Luz pulled me into the living room and sat down on the couch, patting the seat beside her.

"I like practice English," she said. "We talk, okay?"

"Okay," I agreed. "Can you teach me Tagalog? I'd really like to learn."

"Good," Luz nodded. "I teach you, you teach me."

"Can you teach me to cook *adobo* and *pancit* and *lumpia,* too?" I asked.

"*O-o,*" she said.

"What?" I looked around the room, expecting to see a baby falling down or a big lizard climbing the walls. Luz chuckled and clapped her hands.

"*O-o* mean yes."

"Oh," I nodded. *"O-o."*

"Hinde mean no," she continued. I recognized the word from the hotel, where the busboy had been telling me not to drink the water.

"What's *masarap?"* I asked. Both the *balut* man and the bellboy had used the word.

"Masarap—delicious." Luz rubbed her tummy. "You remember good." She leaned forward and whispered, "Now you tell me what is frofilactic?"

"I never heard that word," I said. "Where did you hear it?"

"I went to doctor today," Luz said. "Nurse say Filipinas should use frofilactic, but she don't tell me what it means."

"You're not sick, are you?" I was concerned.

"Oh, no," Luz laughed. "I fregnant. In six month, I going to have new baby," she said proudly.

Then I knew what frofilactic meant, but I remembered the papers I signed in the air terminal, saying that I didn't bring any birth control into the country.

"I know what you mean now," I told Luz. "You mean prophylactic."

"Right!" she said. "What that means?"

"Uh . . . it's just something people use so they don't get pregnant," I said, hoping she wouldn't ask how you use it. Luz wasn't interested in how to use such a device; she didn't understand why anyone would want to avoid pregnancy.

"Who don't want be fregnant?" She frowned. "Is why women born, right?" She sat back and patted her tiny tummy. "Man works, woman have babies."

"Well, sometimes women work and they don't want to have babies for a while."

"Poor ladies." Luz looked sad. "Have to work. But someday they get married and have babies. Don't have to work

185

so hard." She looked at me. "Why you don't have husband? You pretty."

"Thank you," I said. "But I want to travel for a while and have a career before I settle down."

"I travel, too." Luz beamed. "We go to United States of America someday. I will be citizen." She sat looking into space for a minute, imagining herself in the States. She reached over and patted my leg. "Don't worry," she said with a serious look, "I teach you cook good. Then somebody marry you and you have babies, too."

We had so much fun talking and comparing our lives that it was late when we woke up Jep to drive me back to the barracks.

"We can't drive now," he said. "It's after midnight."

"Why not?" I said.

"It's because of the martial law. There's a curfew," he said. "You have to have a curfew pass to be on the streets between midnight and four A.M. If you don't, the police will throw you in jail. Believe me, you don't want to be in jail here." He got up off the bed and yawned as he stretched his arms over his head.

"Why don't you stay here?" he asked. "We have an extra room that we use for the kids to play in."

"Are you sure it's all right?"

"Oh, lucky!" Luz hopped up and down and clapped her hands. "American girl sleep in our house!" She ran to put clean sheets on the bed.

"She'll be a celebrity tomorrow," Jep said. "Her friends are crazy about American women." He carried my seabag and my *balut* into the bedroom.

"You're really going native, aren't you?" he said, holding up the bag of eggs at arm's length. "Even Luz won't eat these things. I can smell them from here."

"I'm sending them as an Easter gift to a friend who has

unique taste," I said. Luz giggled as she finished tucking in the sheets and fluffed up the pillow.

"Well, I hope I'm not on your gift list." Jep set the bag down in the far corner of the room and stopped to pull the straw window shade down. "Make yourself at home," he said on his way out of the room. "You're welcome to stay as long as you want to." Luz waited until Jep left the room, then squeezed my hand with a bashful smile.

"Magandang gabi," she whispered. "Good night, my new friend."

"Magandang gabi."

14

"One-Take Johnson"

Jep drove me to the barracks on the way home from work the next day. He talked to the barracks manager while I filled out the necessary forms. Instead of handing me a room key and a stack of linens as I expected, the Air Force sergeant behind the desk gave me another form.

"Get your CO's autograph on this and you're in business," he said.

"What's this?" I glanced at the paper in my hand. It was a request for permission to live off base.

"That's your invitation to stay in our guest room," Jep grinned. "Unless, of course, you'd rather stay here."

"Are you serious?" I asked.

Jep nodded. "Luz and I already discussed it. She really likes you."

"I like her, too," I said. "But you have to let me pay my share of the rent."

Jep frowned and closed his eyes. "Let me see," he said. "One quarter is one hundred pesos, divided by eight." He opened his eyes. "That comes to twelve-fifty."

"Twelve-fifty what?" He had lost me somewhere.

"Twelve dollars and fifty cents per month," Jep said.

I did a brief mental calculation. "You mean you pay fifty dollars for a four-bedroom house?" It was too incredible to believe.

"It's three hundred and fifty pesos," Jep said. "To a Filipino, that's quite a bit of money." He offered his hand. "Do we have a deal?"

"It's a deal." As we shook hands, I rattled the request form. "Will the CO sign this? After that fiasco at the station last night he probably hates me."

Jep took the request, folded it, and put it in his pocket. "I'll take care of it."

That evening, I became an official resident of Old Balibago, Pampanga. Luz was thrilled to have a live-in tutor and I welcomed the opportunity to live the native life.

At first, Lydia and Marites refused to let me do any work around the house. To them, there was nothing unique about boiling water to wash dishes or taking cold showers; they had never seen hot running water. They didn't understand why I thought it was fun to fetch a five-pound block of ice from the corner store or wash clothes by hand. For several weeks, they rolled their eyes and giggled at my clumsy attempts to mimic their actions, but when they realized that I truly wanted to adopt the Filipino lifestyle, they welcomed my help with the chores and took great delight in my progress. Before long, I could wrap an eggroll with the best of them.

I had so much fun playing native that I sometimes had to force myself to go to work, although I liked my new job as much as my new lifestyle. The hectic pace of the broadcasting station was exhilarating and I got a kick out of watching the videotapes of myself making the weather reports on live television.

Every day, on the way to AFPN-TV, I stopped at the Air Operations building to pick up the latest weather forecasts. The Air Ops was a squat gray building located at the base of the air control tower. From outside, it looked like any other drab military building. Inside, it was another story. On my way to the back of the building to pick up the teletype reports, I passed the radar room. Entrance to the room was restricted to authorized personnel who sat in front of strange machines that bleeped and blooped mysteriously in the eerie green glow of the radar screens.

Next to the radar room was the ward room, a sanctuary for pilots and navigators, strictly off limits to those unfortunate souls who depended on feet and wheels for transportation and wore boring clothes instead of spiffy green flight suits and nifty sunglasses. Night and day, the ward room was filled with aviators playing acey-deucey on backgammon boards. They played with fierce concentration, as though their reputation as pilots was based more on their ability to play acey-deucey than on their skill in piloting aircraft. I often overheard one pilot describe another's masterful command of the acey-deucey board, but the only time they ever commented on each other's flying talents was if a pilot pulled off a daring stunt like doing a barrel roll while flying over the chief of staff's office or landing a plane with its wheels up.

Outside the ward room was a series of giant wall maps, covered with arrows, lines, and squiggles which pilots claimed to be able to interpret as flight patterns that indicated the best way to fly from here to there and back again. I was never absolutely convinced that pilots could actually read the charts. I secretly believed that their special aviator sunglasses allowed them to look at the maps without seeing the arrows, lines, and squiggles, so they could get a general idea of the direction they needed to fly to reach Chicago or China.

The teletype machines sat in a line against the back wall of the building, humming and zapping out the latest weather forecasts. Above the machines was a row of clocks, each one set for a different time zone. The biggest clock, in the center, was labeled "GMT" for Greenwich Mean Time. Greenwich, England, apparently, is the only place in the world where people live in the present. Everyone else lives in GMT plus or minus some number of hours.

When I picked up the afternoon forecast, I usually checked the Eastern Standard Time clock to see what time it was back home. Tuesday in the Philippines is Monday in Pennsylvania. I promised my family that, since I was living a day ahead of them, I'd be sure to call and let them know if the world ended. That way, they'd have one final day to squeeze in some last-minute fun and prayer.

I always looked behind me to make sure the coast was clear before I bent under the counter to tear off the reports. The rear section of the building was always deserted by late afternoon, but the teletype machines were located under a long, low counter and I had to hike my straight skirt up a few inches, so I could reach under the counter. It made me self-conscious, even though I knew that any pilot still on base had already checked the forecasts and been off into the wild blue yonder and back again to the acey-deucey tables.

Whack! As I reached down to tear off a report one day, I felt a sharp smack across my bottom. My elbow hit the edge of the counter, sending a sharp tingle up my arm, as I turned to face an unfamiliar Air Force captain posing in the doorway. The tag on the pocket of his flight suit said his name was "Smooch." Smooch leaned against the door frame, crossed one baggy green leg in front of the other, and twirled his sunglasses in the air.

I gave him a haughty look. "I beg your pardon, sir," I said, as I massaged my elbow. "I neither invite nor appreciate that kind of attention. Don't do it again." Still twirling his sunglasses, Smooch shrugged and disappeared around the corner.

Disgusted with my cowardice, I slammed the reports on the counter top. "I beg your pardon," I fumed, mimicking myself. "What a wimp! I should have told him off. I should have punched old Captain Smooch right in the eye." As I yanked the last report out of the machine, I felt another whack—this one even harder than the first. I dropped the report, clenched my fist, and swung my right arm as fast and hard as I could. My aim was perfect; I caught Captain Smooch in the side of the head, crushing my hand against his ear and the top of his jawbone. Stunned, he rubbed his cheek where my heavy ring had left a satisfying indentation.

"Don't you know you can get a court-martial for striking a commissioned officer, Wave?" He glared at me as the red flush spread from his ear across his angry face.

I took a deep breath and scowled back at him. "You hit me first," I said, hoping his ears were still ringing loud enough to prevent him from hearing my knees knocking. "That's aggravated assault, any way you slice it, *sir!*" With a dignified toss of my head, I collected my papers, walked outside, and collapsed against the side of the building. Even though I knew I was right and he didn't have a case against me, it was still a traumatic experience to punch an officer in the head. His threat to court-martial me would have scared me out of my wits if I hadn't remembered Chief Bagget's advice.

"When an officer steps out of line, he steps on his own tail, Johnson," the chief had told me. "Remember that."

I remembered it. I also remembered how Commander Wadsworth, my executive officer, had harassed me at my first duty station until I finally stood up to him. I didn't get busted for my bravery; I got a dozen red roses.

I knew Captain Smooch wouldn't be able to get me in trouble, either, because he hit me first, and maybe he'd think twice before he smacked another woman. I guess I showed him, all right. I stood up, straightened my cap, and headed for the post office to pick up my mail on the way to the station.

Dear Skunk Breath,

Thanks so much for the exquisite Easter eggs. I can't begin to tell you how much I appreciate your thoughtfulness and good taste. It's a gift I will always remember, mainly because one of them broke on my desk, which now smells (permanently, I fear) like a very dead egg. Of course, you don't need to worry. I'm sure I'll think of a way to show my overwhelming gratitude for your lovely gift.

Lucky for you, I'm in a magnanimous mood because I was recently engaged to Tony, my favorite sailor. He has another year to go on board his carrier, so I extended my enlistment for a year. That way I can finish up my bachelor's degree before we get married and go live in New England, where people know how to talk right (and don't send disgusting presents to their pals who have always been true friends to them).

I was gonna invite you to the wedding, but now I'm not so sure. I really owe you a big one, but maybe if you buy us a real expensive present like a yacht or an Italian sports car I'll let you off the hook.

Your Former Pal,
Lucas

Jep was right about Big Al Stratter minding his manners—and keeping his pants on—after my first night as the weather lady. When I wasn't busy writing spot announcements, Stratter or his assistant Bud Kruger, an Air Force staff sergeant, kept me on camera, announcing the daily community interest and military news programs that were videotaped and replayed twice a day.

Kruger told me I was pretty good for a rookie. He was

a real pro who handled a microphone as well as he handled a camera, so a compliment from him meant a lot to me, especially since I wanted to make sure I was ready when my turn came to anchor the news. I knew I could do a good job in the anchor spot. I never had to yell, "Cut!" and make the engineers rewind the videotape when I was taping a show. Some of the guys needed seven or eight takes just to complete a five-minute recording, but the engineers called me "One-Take Johnson."

Kruger had a nasty red scar under his chin that he rubbed a lot when he was thinking. He never talked about that scar, though. He wasn't the talkative type. He wasn't the nervous type, either. Once, Kruger was operating a camera when a light crashed down off the ceiling and started a fire behind the set during a live interview with the base commander, a full colonel in the Air Force.

Commander Willenbrau, who had come to observe the interview and rub elbows with the colonel, started bouncing off the walls in the control room, swearing and pounding his fist into his palm. His panic infected the crew and everyone froze—except Kruger, of course. Kruger locked his camera, set his cigar on top of it, walked calmly over to the fire extinguisher, and put out the small flame. Then he switched on a different light and went back to his camera and cigar. The colonel was having so much fun watching himself on the TV monitor in front of the set that he never even noticed the excitement.

Nothing went on the air at AFPN-TV or Radio that Commander Willenbrau didn't notice, even in the middle of the night. Besides the TV and the radio in his office, he had four radios and three TV's in his house, including one of each in his bathroom, so he could supervise even while perched on the john. Once, when I was on duty at one o'clock in the morning, a fly landed on the projector during a rerun of an old western movie. I thought it was amusing. It looked like the fly was riding a horse across the prairie. The fly didn't ride two yards before the CO was on the phone screaming at me, as though I could watch the clock, read the broadcast schedule, operate the switcher, swat flies, and listen to him scream at the same time.

Another time, the film broke while I was showing a three-reel movie. I ran back to splice the film, forgetting, in my haste, to put up the slide of a smiling pineapple that said PLEASE STAND BY. WE ARE HAVING TECHNICAL DIFFICULTIES.

When the red phone rang, I dropped the film and answered it.

"What the hell's going on over there?" The CO's voice jangled my ear drum. "Put the goddam slide on the screen, you dipshit!" I dropped the phone and put the slide into the film chain. I could hear the CO screaming even louder—I had put the slide in upside down. I fixed the slide, then picked up the film and tried to splice it. The whole time, the CO was serenading me so I wouldn't get lonely. My hands shook and I dropped the reel on the floor, where it rolled around my feet, unwinding as it traveled. Commander Willenbrau was shrieking so loud that I was afraid he'd have a stroke. As I reached for the phone with one hand and frantically tried to rewind the film with my other hand, Kruger strolled into the control room, took a look around, and puffed up a cloud of smoke. Then he picked up the phone, said, "Catch you later, sir," and hung up. He slapped a piece of masking tape over the break and had the film back on the air in thirty seconds.

"Relax," he said, as he sat down in front of the switcher. "The Old Man likes to holler, but he's harmless." He leaned back and put his feet on top of the control panel and tapped the ashes from his palm. Carefully, he reached over and rubbed the ashes into one of his socks. I couldn't help staring at him.

"Gotta keep the equipment clean," he said. He puffed in silence for a minute, then looked at me and said, "CO tried that screaming crap with me once. I invited him to show me how to do the job." He snorted, "Shit! He doesn't even know to turn a projector on. That's the last time he called when I was on duty."

Kruger wasn't one of those guys who pretend to be tough. He really was tough. I knew how he got that scar on his neck. He had only been assigned to the station for a year on unaccompanied orders, which meant that he couldn't bring his wife. The Air Force wouldn't ship a whole family and household around the world just for a one-year assignment, so Kruger was on his own.

Kruger wasn't bad looking and, with his self-confidence, probably never had a problem finding female company. But in the Philippines, even unattractive American men, who lacked either the personality, the courage, or the appearance to attract women in the States, suddenly found that there were plenty of pretty young girls who were eager to keep them company—for the right price. With the favorable exchange rate, the right price was pretty cheap. For a few dollars a month, a man could rent a place and have a live-in cook, laundress, and playmate.

Kruger set himself up with an apartment and a girl off base, but, since he was not an emotional man, he overlooked the fact that his hired girlfriend had feelings like any other woman. Ignoring her objections, he openly carried on his flirtations and flings. One morning, Kruger breezed into his apartment after a night on the town with a cocktail waitress. His girlfriend met him at the door. When he walked in, she slit his throat with a bolo knife.

A crueler man might have punched her; a weaker one

might have passed out. Kruger simply turned around and walked outside and down the street to use the telephone in a nearby bar. He called the station and told Jep, who was on duty, that he had had a little accident and would appreciate a ride to the hospital. Jep called the dispensary and got someone else to handle the control room so he could ride with the ambulance. When they arrived at the apartment, Jep and the paramedics found Kruger sitting on the front steps, puffing on a cigar, holding his throat together with his free hand.

After that experience, most men would have moved back to the barracks and mended their adulterous ways, but not Kruger. As soon as he got out of the hospital, he rented another apartment and hired a new girlfriend. I heard the CO talking to Kruger about the incident. The CO wanted Kruger to press charges against the girl who cut him, but he refused.

"Shit!" Kruger told the CO. "If I was her, I would have aimed a lot lower."

For his girlfriend's sake, I was glad that Kruger didn't press charges. Luz had told me how hard life could be for poor Filipinas. Most of them ended up working as maids or housegirls, she said, but many naive young girls, some barely in their teens, were tricked into becoming hookers. Pimps would buy pretty new clothes for a group of prostitutes and pay them a lot of money to take a little vacation. They'd take the prostitutes to a distant barrio or out to one of the smaller islands, where the girls would impress the villagers with their imported clothes and tales of the good life, rubbing elbows with rich Americans. The gullible farmers would believe that their daughters were being hired to work in an office, where they'd have the opportunity to meet Americans and, perhaps, marry them and go to the U.S., where they'd become citizens and enjoy a class of living which their hard-working fathers could never hope to provide.

Once the girls arrived in Olongapo City, outside the Navy base, they would find that they'd been hired to sell their favors to sailors on liberty. With no money, no family or friends, and unable to speak the local dialect, they had few options. Even if there were a way to return to their villages, they were too ashamed. Their family names would be ruined. No one would want a woman who had been hired as a prostitute, even if she had never worked to earn the title.

"That makes me sick! Tell me it isn't true," I said, though I knew it probably was. I hadn't lived in the P.I. very long, but I'd been there long enough to know that the women were easily exploited. "How could they believe such a crazy story?"

"Some people do crazy thing to have chance go to America," Luz said with a shrug. We sat on stools in the backyard, helping Lydia wring out a bucket full of dripping clothes. Looking at Luz, it was hard to believe that she had just had a baby a few days ago. She hadn't gained more than ten pounds during the months I'd lived at her house. Instead of eating like a horse and waddling through her pregnancy, Luz had quietly gone about her business.

One night, Jep and I came home from the station to find Jep Junior gurgling in the bed beside Luz. There was no phone to call Jep when she went into labor, so Lydia, Marites, and Grandma Lola delivered the baby, cleaned the house, and cooked dinner. To them, childbirth was so natural that they didn't understand why Americans worried so much about it.

"Baby know how be born." Luz smiled at my silly worries and nuzzled the top of Junior's head. "When he ready, he come out." After two days in bed, resting, Luz was back on her feet, slim and energetic, helping Lydia and me wash the clothes. Lydia washed them by hand in a big tub with a bar of soap and a brush, inside a little mosquito-infested shed behind the house, and then carried them to us for rinsing and wringing in another tub. The method was quite primitive, but I never heard the women complain. It was what they had always done. Once, I asked Luz if she had ever used a washing machine. She arched her eyebrows and gave me a condescending look.

"Machine don't get clothes really clean like hand does," she informed me. "Is better you see dirt wash out."

The Filipina women thought I was crazy, but I was fascinated by their chores. Instead of whipping out the sponge mop and spreading a bottle of acrylic floor polish on the gleaming red tiles, Marites would "coconut" the floor. After she and Lydia scrubbed it on their hands and knees with brushes, they rinsed off every trace of soap and dried the floor with rags before applying paste wax with a cotton pad. Then Marites took half a coconut shell and set it on the floor. With one bare foot gripping the shell, she hopped around the floor and whisked the coconut back and forth, leaving a glossy path in her wake. The floor looked marvelous, but the coconut-flavored wax attracted hundreds of ants. When I mentioned them to Marites, she said, "That why wash floor every day. Get rid of ant."

"If you didn't spread coconut crumbs all over the floor, you wouldn't have ants," I said.

"If no coconut, how you shine floor?" Marites asked, shaking her head and rolling her eyes at Lydia and Luz, who giggled at my ignorance.

They all knew I was not quite right, mentally, because they had seen me, with their own eyes, lying outside in the sun, wearing a swimsuit. One balmy Saturday afternoon,

I put on my swimsuit and picked a nice soft spot in the backyard to read a book and work on my suntan. A three-foot fence surrounded the yard, so silly me thought there'd be little chance of anyone seeing me on the ground.

I hadn't been outside ten minutes before I heard whispers coming from the bushes that bordered the fence. I looked up to see ten brown faces peering over the fence at me.

"*Katakataka!*" one woman hissed to another.

"*Talaga!*" the other woman answered. Neither of them took their eyes off me during the exchange.

Five more faces joined the throng and I could hear more people coming down the street.

"What's the matter?" I yelled, grabbing my beach towel and running towards the house. "Is it against the law to lie in the backyard?"

Luz heard me shouting and met me at the back door. When she appeared, everyone in the crowd began chattering at once. I had learned quite a few words in Tagalog, but I didn't understand a word Luz said to them.

"What's wrong?" I asked her. "Haven't they ever seen anyone get a suntan before?"

"No." Luz smiled at me. "Women here not go outside with no clothes."

"I have clothes on!" I said. "This is a swimming suit and it isn't a very revealing one at that."

"We no wear swimming suit," Luz explained.

"Well, what do you wear when you go swimming?"

"We no go swimming," she said. "Sometimes go to beach, but wear clothes in water so skin don't get more brown."

"Your skin is beautiful," I said. "I wish I had a built-in suntan like you." I nodded at the people who were still staring over the fence. "Look how pretty their skin is, it's so smooth and golden brown."

Luz looked at them for a minute, as if seeing their skin for the first time. "They don't think brown skin pretty. Brown skin come from work in rice field." She touched my arm. "Light skin mean very high class. Mean you have Spanish ancestor."

She spoke to the group and I could tell from their bashful smiles that she told them I thought they were pretty. One slender young girl, apparently unaware of the beauty of her delicate features, asked Luz a question in a lilting voice. Luz looked at me and shrugged her shoulders.

"What?" I asked.

"She wants to know if she can touch your skin," Luz said.

The request was so unexpected, I didn't answer for a few seconds.

Luz thought I was afraid. "She not hurt you," she said.

"Why not?" I said, wrapping the towel around me, suddenly modest. "But let me go put on a T-shirt and a pair of shorts first. I'm beginning to feel undressed." Luz spoke to the girl as I got up and picked up my towel. As I turned around to walk into the house, the girl asked another question. I looked at Luz, who clapped her hand over her mouth and giggled.

"Come on," I said. "What did she ask you?"

"She ask me ask you how you get butt so nice and fat," Luz said between chuckles.

"Ha!" I laughed, recalling the many times I had watched with envy as a slim-hipped Filipina walked by.

"Ask her to put that in writing," I said. "I know at least a million American women who would appreciate hearing that point of view."

It doesn't rain for five or six months in the P.I., but then the rains make up for lost time by pouring down for weeks without stopping. After a few days, everything outside either sinks or floats. After thirty-six days of rain without a break, I could feel the mildew growing under my fingernails and behind my ears. But aside from the fact that I had to leave the house barefoot and wade to the car and from the car to the station, carrying my pantyhose and shoes and the knowledge that I was constantly in danger of getting a concussion from a flying coconut in the seventy-mile-an-hour winds during a typhoon, I didn't mind the rain all that much. At least I got to change the weather report on the evening news. Now, instead of sticking little pictures of sunshine on the local map, I stuck little tornado-shaped clouds along the path of the latest storm.

When the rains began so did the mah jong tournaments. Luz and Lydia would challenge Lola and Marites to a game in the kitchen. They were serious competitors, placing their bets with the skill of hard-core poker players. Wives of other servicemen would splash across the street to join the game, betting the money they earned on the black market by selling their monthly quota of eight cartons of American cigarettes from the base exchange. On the street, the women often made ten or fifteen dollars' profit per carton.

Luz refused to sell anything on the black market, because Jep could get in trouble and she might be prevented from moving to the States with him. She didn't need to sell cigarettes, anyway. The pile of money usually ended up in front of her seat at the mah jong table.

While the mah jong masters clicked their colorful game tiles in the kitchen, I studied in the living room, humming along to the tune of the rain pattering on the banana leaves outside. In addition to my regular college courses, I was preparing for my second-class petty officer exam. It would probably take about six months for the test results to be published, and by that time I'd be ready to move into the anchor spot on the evening news.

At AFPN, each broadcaster spent a few months in continuity, writing announcements and scripts, then worked as a disc jockey in radio production. After a stint in the newsroom, taping remote broadcasts of the sporting events and political commentary programs that kept overseas Americans entertained and informed, came the chance to work in the more visible and glamorous world of television production. Each time I moved to a new assignment, I tried extra hard to learn everything quickly and well, because I was the first woman some of the men had ever worked with and I wanted them to have a good attitude towards the next woman, as well as respect for my professional ability.

When I moved into TV production, I started out on the night shift. Jep was on day shift, so he lent me his car for the three-mile drive to the base. Because of the curfew, I had to carry a curfew pass with me to show that I had official permission to be on the streets of Balibago after midnight.

Usually, the streets were deserted at three o'clock in the morning, and I bounced along the winding dirt road, dodging potholes in a sleepy haze. There were no street lights off base, so I didn't see the man dressed in black and wearing a black ball-cap step out of the shadows until he was close enough to touch the hood of the car. He held up his right hand, motioning me to stop. I slowed down until I saw that his left hand held a stick twice the size of a baseball bat. With a shriek, I stepped on the gas and raced toward Jep's house. As I took off, the man blew three shrill blasts on a whistle and I could see other men rushing from the shadows to join him. They all carried big sticks and wore black ball-caps.

"If this is some new version of baseball," I said to myself as I gripped the steering wheel and squealed around a tight corner, "it would be easier if they just bought a ball, instead of trying to knock my head off in the middle of the night." I screeched into the driveway with the men close behind. I locked the car doors and lay on the horn, beeping frantically. The men surrounded the car and I prayed they wouldn't smash the windows and kill me on the spot. The man who had tried to stop me walked up and tapped on the glass, but I closed my eyes and screamed, pounding my fists on the car horn.

It wasn't long before Jep ran out into the night, wearing his boxer shorts and waving a bolo knife in the air. I could see Luz standing in the doorway and Lola peering over her shoulder.

"Get out of here before I call the police!" Jep yelled.

"We are folice!" the man standing beside the car shouted. "We are *baranguay* folice."

"The hell you are!" Jep took a step towards the man, but Luz ran out and pulled on his arm. She spoke quickly, gesturing towards the men and shaking her head. Jep lowered the knife, but stood ready to attack as Luz approached the man. He pulled a piece of paper out of his pocket and she looked at it and nodded. She pointed to me and to her house, apparently explaining that I lived there.

"Is okay come out, Luana!" she shouted to me. "Is really folice."

I rolled the window down a little, but didn't open the door. "If they're police, how come they're wearing baseball uniforms and carrying bats?" I asked, keeping my eye on the leader of the team.

"*Baranguay* folice special," Luz explained. 'Take turn to watch streets at night while wife, children sleep." As she spoke, the men walked over to join the leader, whistles bouncing against their chests. When I looked at them, they smiled at me to show their good will.

"You just show curfew fass and everything fine," Luz said. "Come on."

After checking to make sure that Jep was still on guard with his bolo knife, I slowly opened the car door, ready to slam it shut if any of the men made a move. My hands were shaking so hard that I dropped my purse on the ground while I was trying to find my curfew pass. Luz picked it up and pulled out the laminated yellow square of paper. She held it up so the vigilante baseball police could see it and I took a few steps closer to Jep. Even though the men acted friendly, I wanted Jep and his bolo knife between them and me.

Satisfied with my credentials, the men straightened their hats and prepared to leave. The leader spoke to Luz and she turned to me.

"He say next time you stop when he blow whistle."

"Sure," I agreed. "I'll stop." As long as they were pretending to be policemen, I figured I could pretend to believe them. If I ever saw them again, I'd turn around and head back towards the base, where the military policemen wear white hats and carry guns.

15

Outranked
and Outraged

Luz believed that the U.S. Constitution guaranteed the right of every woman to have a driver's license. She asked Jep to teach her to drive before they moved to the States, but he told her that only a crazy man would try to teach a Filipina to drive a car, especially if he wanted to stay married to her.

"I'm crazy," I told Luz. "I'll teach you." Delighted, Luz hugged herself, twirled around on her tiptoes, and hugged me.

I suggested the idea to Jep that evening as we drove home from work, but he didn't appreciate my offer. He banged on the steering wheel and ranted for a while, then brooded silently until we reached the house.

"Oh, go ahead and teach her," he said, as we pulled into the driveway. He got out of the car and slammed the dented door. "You can't damage this old car. And it's your nervous breakdown." He walked into the house and headed for the kitchen.

"Jep . . ." I followed him inside, shaking my finger at him. "I'm surprised at you. Luz isn't a child and you usually don't treat her like one." Barefoot, Luz ran noiselessly up to the back door, but she stopped outside the screen door when she heard us talking about her precious driving lessons. Jep had his back to the door and didn't see her wink at me and press her finger to her lips.

"Shee!" Jep yanked open the ice box and took out a bottle of San Miguel beer. "I know Luz isn't a child, but Filipinas don't drive," he insisted. After a couple of sips from the bottle, his usual good humor returned. With a mischievous look, he pulled out another beer and offered it to me. "Want one? The ice is all melted, so it's just the way you like it—lukewarm," he said.

I stuck out my tongue and clutched my throat. He knew all about my traumatic introduction to life in the islands. After that first, unforgettable sleepless night in a hotel room full of lizards, with a bathroom full of roaches and a bladder full of San Miguel, Jep knew I'd rather have a root canal than a bottle of beer.

Jep watched me stagger around the kitchen for a few seconds, then interrupted my death scene, suddenly serious. "I'm not trying to keep Luz from learning things, you know," he said. "But she wasn't raised to drive cars. She didn't even go to high school. Most of the women here don't, unless they're rich and Westernized. The only things girls in this country learn to do is cook, clean, and have babies. They don't understand anything about engines or gears or traffic laws."

Indignant on Luz's behalf, I huffed, "Any woman who can take care of an old lady, a live-in friend, and two babies that she gave birth to in her bedroom in between household chores and who can cook gourmet meals on a two-burner stove with bottled gas, play an unbeatable game of mah jong, and keep her darling husband so happy"—I wrinkled my nose at Jep—"can certainly learn to operate a simple machine like a car."

Jep finished his beer with a slurp. Forcing a belch, he rubbed his flat belly. "Go ahead and ruin mah woman," he drawled. "Ah don't care." Luz hadn't made a sound until then, but she couldn't suppress a chuckle when Jep did his cowboy imitation. Jep wheeled around, ran to the door, and swooped Luz up into his arms. She screamed with delight as he carried her inside, rubbing his stubbly chin on her neck.

"Spying on me, were you?" he growled. Luz, undaunted, kissed his nose.

"Trying to soften me up so I'll let you use my car to learn to drive, huh?"

"Yes!" Luz squealed.

"And if I say no, you'll drive me crazy, won't you?" he asked.

"Yes!"

"Okay." Jep set her down gently and looked at me. "Just be careful with mah little lady," he said.

Little was right. Luz couldn't see over the steering wheel in Jep's station wagon. Her head was level with the horn, until we propped her up on some couch cushions. Then she could see over the wheel, but she couldn't reach the gas and brake pedals. We compromised on a position where she could peek between the steering wheel and the dashboard and still reach the pedals. She was determined to learn to drive, since Jep had finally given in and promised to buy her a compact car if she earned her driver's license before they were transferred back to the States. Jep wasn't due to transfer for a year, but Luz was anxious to start practicing immediately.

I'd drive through town with Luz, and when we reached the deserted one-lane dirt road outside of town we'd trade places. I watched for children, chickens, water buffalo, and potholes while Luz gripped the steering wheel with white knuckles and concentrated on staying on the road. After practicing every day for a few weeks, Luz was ready to drive through town and off in the opposite direction from our usual course.

We bumped along for several miles before we reached

a small village. Beside the road, women bent over what looked like large pieces of velvety brown cloth, thrashing the cloth with sticks and brooms. The women were dressed in long, flowing dresses, with straw hats tied to their heads. "What are they doing?" I asked Luz. She stopped to look out the window. "They cleaning rice," she announced. I looked closer and saw that the brown cloth was really rice, with the outer sheath of the grain still intact. It was a revelation to me, who grew up believing that rice was white and came in boxes.

The village consisted of ten *nipa* huts, thatched houses woven from *nipa*-palm leaves. To avoid floods during the rainy season and wild animals during the dry season, the houses were all built on tall stilts. As we drove by, I noticed a small boy sleeping on the back of a very large water buffalo, a *carabao*, that was tied to the stilt supporting one of the houses. The *carabao* could easily have walked off, toppling the house, but he stood placidly blinking, his head swaying gently to and fro, as though rocking the child asleep on his back. It tickled me to see that *carabao* standing so peacefully, indulging his owner's belief that he was a captive animal.

Past the village, the vegetation grew denser as we approached the mountain jungles. The humidity was so high that it felt as if I could grab a handful of air and wring the water out of it. Luz was too busy driving to talk and the sun baked my face, lulling me to sleep in spite of the bumpy ride. When the bumping suddenly stopped, I woke up. We had stopped in the middle of the empty road.

"What's the matter?" I sat up straight and rubbed my eyes. Luz was staring straight ahead through the windshield.

"We lost," she whispered, without turning her head.

I looked at my watch and realized we had been driving

for less than two hours. Considering the condition of the road and Luz's careful speed, we couldn't have gone more than forty or fifty miles. "How can we be lost? This road only goes in one direction."

"No." Luz looked at me, her big eyes shining with unshed tears. "I take turn while you sleep. Want to surprise you." She sniffed. "Big surprise! Now we lost!"

"Don't worry." I patted her arm. "We'll just ask directions from the next person we see."

After driving another fifteen minutes, Luz slowed down. "People live here," she said.

I looked out the window at the banana trees and coconut palms. "I don't see anyone."

Luz pointed to the mountain side. "Someone build house," she said. Following her hand, I saw a large piece of rusty corrugated metal propped up with sticks.

"That's a house?" I was appalled. "That hunk of metal?"

"That man probably live there," Luz said, looking out her window at an old man approaching across a rice field, wearing only a straw hat and a rag tied around his body, Tarzan-style.

Luz got out of the car and walked to the edge of the field to meet him. After a few brief words, she got back into the car. "He not know there another town," she said, matter of factly.

"How can he not know where the next town is?"

"He not know there another town," Luz repeated.

"You mean he doesn't know which direction it is, don't you?" I asked.

"No. He not know there another town anywhere," Luz explained. "He just know this where he live."

"You mean he lives under a hunk of metal on the edge of a jungle and doesn't even know there is another place in the whole world?" I stared at the man as he shuffled on towards his hut. "That poor man!"

"He not know he poor," Luz pointed out. "He very happy. Have wife, children, grandchildren, *carabao*, chickens, banana, mango. Roof keep rain off head. Why he need other things?" She looked at me with her wise eyes and I frowned until I began to understand what she was telling me.

"You mean like he isn't missing anything by not having taxes and crime and rent?"

"Right," Luz nodded as she started the car. "He just have happy life."

After another thirty nervous minutes of driving in the dusty heat, we recognized a familiar barrio.

Luz sighed in relief. "Now we be home soon."

Only a few dozen miles separated us from that old man, but I knew I could drive forever and I'd still never come close to reaching his world.

When I told them the good news about my promotion to second-class petty officer, Luz and Marites planned a fiesta. The entire neighborhood was invited and everyone wore their brightest clothes. The men brought their pet chickens and staged a cock fight while they barbecued a whole roast pig in the back yard. The women fried platters of pork fat into crispy *chichirron*, rolled hundreds of *lumpia* egg rolls, and fixed lots of interesting, unrecognizable dishes that were too delicious to spoil by asking what the ingredients were. Fish of every size and shape were also served, complete with their heads. The fish were delicious, but I had to eat with my eyes closed. I had a hard time eating something that looked back at me, even if it was dead and fried.

Their voices rising above the squawking poultry, the children performed folk dances and songs in the street. Marites's brothers brought two long bamboo poles to use for *tinikling*, a dance performed by hopping between the poles. The two boys squatted, holding the bamboo parallel to the ground while one of the children danced barefoot between the sticks, hopping and kicking as the boys clicked the poles together and tapped them on the ground in an intricate rhythm.

The dance started out slowly, speeding up until the child's feet became a dancing blur that flashed above and between the poles until finally the boys clapped the bamboo on the ground with a final flourish. It looked easy, so I took my turn and managed to last about five minutes before I fell over, breathless, with one foot still between the poles. The crowd pronounced me *mabuti naman*—pretty good.

Meanwhile, back at the station, Commander Willenbrau was making his own plans to celebrate my promotion, but it wasn't a fiesta. Instead, he told me I'd have to wait for a few months before I got to be the anchor person on the news because he had an exciting new project for me. My assignment was to develop a women's feature television program. The new project kept me busy, researching stories, writing scripts, desiging the set, producing the introduction, taking photos for slides to be used on the show. I designed and helped build the set, then took my place in front of the camera, welcoming the audience to "Woman's World." Each show had a different theme—women in science, women in medicine, women in sports. The CO said the shows were good, but he didn't schedule them for immediate broadcast. He said he wanted to have a whole series taped before we started showing them.

Kruger wasn't as naive as I was. He pointed out the fact that some of the junior men were being assigned to the anchor spots while I was busy writing stories offering advice to women on career advancement, education, and professional opportunities. I had followed the same job progression as everyone else on the staff, but men with much less experience and training were moving ahead of me.

"It's no skin off my teeth," Kruger said, "it's just the principle." He bit off the end of a cigar and spat the tobacco off the end of his tongue. "I figure you pay your dues, you ought to get what's coming to you, man or woman, instead of wasting your time on some program that will never be aired."

I looked up from the script I was reading. "What do you mean, never be aired?" I asked Kruger. "I just spent six months of hard work on 'Woman's World.' The CO is going to schedule them after I have a whole series on tape." Kruger shook his head slowly as I spoke.

"Don't quote me, but I figure it this way," he said. "Commander Willenbrau isn't wild about broads in his Navy, so he figures that it'll catch up with him one of these days. When it does, he'll whip out these programs and demonstrate his unbiased support of women. I don't like that one bit. It's too sneaky. I prefer to know who my enemies are right up front."

Kruger's support surprised me. He had always been pleasant to me, but I hadn't realized that I had a friend behind those smelly cigars.

"Wow!" I felt lost, like I'd been driving on the freeway to Pittsburgh and found myself in San Francisco. "What should I do?"

"Don't ask me." Kruger shrugged. "I just thought maybe you'd want to consider the big picture. If I was you, I'd talk to the CO about the situation. You can't win a battle if you don't know what you're fighting for."

I tried to talk to the CO, but every time I approached him, he put me off. He'd schedule an appointment and then have his secretary cancel it at the last minute. I was polite and respectful, until I got my performance evaluation. The CO had described my performance as mediocre, my attitude as uncooperative, and my potential for further advancement as poor. I couldn't believe it. It had to be a mistake, especially after all the extra work I'd been doing. I knocked on Commander Willenbrau's door and walked in before his secretary had a chance to stop me. The CO didn't look a bit surprised. He had been expecting me.

"This isn't right," I said, shaking the report. "It is not a fair evaluation of my performance. I won't sign it."

The CO pursed his lips and clasped his hands under his chin. "It doesn't matter if you sign it or not," he said. "It will just go into your record, noted as unsigned and protested by you."

"But it isn't accurate," I argued. "I've done a good job here. How can you say that I'm a below-average performer?"

"That's the way I see it," he said, "as your commanding officer."

"What about all the extra college classes I've been taking in my free time?" I asked. "And what about the new women's program?"

"Yes, you've spent a lot of time studying for those courses." Commander Willenbrau nodded his head. "And you've spent a lot of time on that extra assignment. Of course, it wasn't an official assignment. Nothing in writing. Maybe you've spent too much time on it and that's why your work suffers occasionally."

"What do you mean, my work suffers?" It took all my control not to shout. "I just got promoted to second-class petty officer! Stratter signed off all my required practical factors. You know he wouldn't sign them off if I couldn't do them." I paused for a minute, but the CO was silent, so I continued. "I've been here almost two years. It's my turn to move into the anchor spot. You know I'm a good broad-caster."

"I don't care if you're the best broadcaster I have, you're not going to anchor a newscast."

"But why not?" I insisted. "Haven't I done a good job on the weather?"

"Yes," the CO nodded.

"So why can't I do the news?"

"Weather isn't real news," he said.

"I do spot news, too. When I tape my women's program, I only need one take. The engineers love me—they call me 'One-Take Johnson.' Lots of the guys stutter and stammer and need ten takes to do one little sixty-second spot."

"Feature programs aren't real news, either," the CO said.

"So what are you gonna do with all those programs I've been taping for the past six months?" I asked. "Aren't you going to air them?"

"That's up to the program manager," the CO said. Kruger was right. Commander Willenbrau was just wasting my time, keeping me busy on projects that would stay on the shelf in the film library.

"Those shows are good," I said. "You know they are."

"You're still not going to anchor the news," the CO repeated.

"Why?" I knew I sounded like a whining kid, trying to convince my mommy to let me stay up late and watch television, but I couldn't help it. The CO was making me crazy, talking in circles. He rearranged the pens on the top of his desk blotter, turning them so the points all faced in the same direction. He spoke to the pens.

"Because I don't believe women have the credibility as announcers to anchor the news. No one will believe you."

"Let me try and see."

"No."

"*Why?*"

The CO realized I wasn't going to give up. He cleared his throat. "Because I don't think women belong in the Navy, that's why." Commander Willenbrau's voice was so low, I could barely hear him. He finished rearranging his pens and then lined up all the papers on his desk. He drummed his fingertips on the desktop for a second, then stood up and walked over to look out the window. "I used to be an enlisted sailor and the women got the shore billets," he said, with his back to me. "I swore that when I became an officer, women weren't going to do men's jobs in my command." When he said that, I realized I was not dealing with a rational man. I tried, desperately, to think of another argument.

"It's against Navy policy to discriminate against women," I said, without conviction, sensing his answer in advance.

"You can't prove it's discrimination." The CO looked up at me, but he didn't smile. He wasn't enjoying his power, just abusing it. "Your performance appraisal is mediocre. In that case, I'm forced to put a junior man ahead of you."

There's a point at which bravery becomes stupidity. I knew it would be stupid to try to fight the CO. An overseas commanding officer has even more power than he would in the States. I could write all the appeals and arguments I wanted to; he would just say I was acting like a typical bitchy broad and the appeals board, men just like him, would believe him.

Suddenly, I was tired, too tired to fight anymore, tired of working so hard for no reward, tired of rain and lizards and roaches and cold showers and not being able to call my mom on Sunday afternoons and—most of all—tired of being told that women couldn't this and women couldn't that. "Okay," I said. "But I don't want to spend two more years as the AFPN weather lady. There's no challenge in telling people that it rains for six months and then doesn't rain for six months. If I can't be an anchor person, I want a transfer back to the States." Commander Willenbrau smiled, without malice.

"In that case, I'm sure I can make a few corrections on your evaluation," he said. "We wouldn't want it to prevent you from advancing in your chosen career." He picked up a red pen and jotted a few notes in the margin of my report, then paused to smile at me again. "I'm glad you're not going to be silly about this. The last woman we had onboard here wasn't as cooperative as you are."

"What happened to her?"

"She's gathering weather reports on Adak Island."

"Adak is off the coast of Alaska, isn't it?" I shuddered just thinking of the frigid weather reports she must be collecting. The CO nodded.

"I see," I said quietly.

"Yes, I'm sure you do."

Luz was thrilled to be able to offer me a ride to the air terminal in her very own car. As we drove through the barrio, I mentally photographed the scenery and tried to memorize the feel of the air and the smells around me— the banana trees, the delicate fragrance of the yellow and white *kalachuchi* flowers, the corner *sari-sari* store with its display of old beer bottles full of pungent fish sauce, tiny children toting blocks of melting ice down the dusty road in their makeshift wagons, the street vendors with their bags of *maiz* and *balut*.

Although I knew I'd miss Jep and Luz and my life in the Philippines, I was eager to return to America, land of hot showers and hamburgers. I knew I'd see Jep and Luz again soon. Jep's new orders put him in charge of the closed-circuit TV system aboard the USS *Kennedy*, which was homeported in Norfolk—just a few miles down the road from the air station where I'd be working as a public affairs specialist.

At the terminal, Luz handed me a package wrapped in brown paper and string. "My brother make this for you," she said, "so you don't forget your home here." Inside was a wooden bowl, made of monkey pod, with carvings of a *carabao* and a *nipa* hut surrounded by banana trees.

She opened my gift as I ran my finger over the delicate carvings, painstakingly etched by a boy who could neither read nor write. "Ooh." Luz sucked in her breath when she saw the metal key chain with her name engraved on the back of a tiny map of the United States. "I had it made for you," I said as I stooped to hug her, "so you can think about your new home." We transferred her keys to the new ring and Luz held it up in the air and gave it a shake.

"Pinakamaganda," she said as the keys jangled. "It mean very most beautiful. Like you, my very most beautiful friend." After one last hug, I picked up my bags and joined the line to check through customs. Luz waited quietly, watching the line of passengers inch forward. Whenever I glanced in her direction, she waved with one hand and clasped the key chain to her chest with the other hand. As I rounded the corner to enter the boarding area, I heard her voice ring out.

"See you in America!"

16

Don't Give
Up the Ship

Four enormous, hairy knuckled hands reached around me and picked up my bags as soon as I pulled them off the ramp at the airport baggage claim in Norfolk. A military policeman stood on either side of me, each decked out in dark blue uniforms with white helmets, white spats, and "MP" armbands. They looked perfectly capable of using their nightsticks to bash in my head, so I let them have my luggage, even though they didn't look like men who would appreciate owning a bagful of lingerie.

"Would you gentlemen mind explaining this unexpected chivalry?" I asked, in the same tone of voice I would have used to address an uncaged orangutan. Neither of them answered, although one of the big bruisers grunted in my general direction.

"Look, fellas," I said. "I appreciate you carrying my luggage, but it isn't really necessary. I can handle it just fine myself." I reached for one of my bags, but the MP intercepted and grabbed my wrist. He toted me and my luggage outside towards a gray Shore Patrol pickup truck parked at the curb. His partner sat in the back of the truck on top of my other suitcase.

When I saw the truck, I finally realized that they intended to arrest me. Under normal circumstances, I would have noticed that fact much earlier, but after traveling for thirty hours nonstop and arriving in the U.S. the day before I left the Philippines, my brain had taken a vacation. In my condition, I could easily have been declared legally asleep.

As the MP towed me towards the truck, I tried to think of a reason why I might be arrested, but the only thing I could think of was that Commander Willenbrau might have seen me give him the finger when I left AFPN. I would have sworn his back was turned, but it wouldn't surprise me at all to find out that he had a tiny television camera installed in the back of his head. He thought I'd forgiven him for his dirty politics just because I accepted the Air Force Commendation Medal he gave me after I applied for a transfer. I would have thrown the medal in his face if I didn't believe that I had honestly earned it. But surely he wouldn't bother to have me arrested just for making an obscene gesture at him.

I tried to wrench my arm free, but the MP had an unbreakable grip on my tender biceps.

"You could at least tell me what's going on," I said. "You can't just go around arresting people without telling them why."

My captor finally found his tongue and grunted, "We're just following orders."

"Well, who gave you the orders?" I asked. No answer. He must have used up his ration of intelligible speech for the day. His daily muscle supply certainly wasn't waning, though. He walked quickly and easily, with my suitcase in one hand and me in the other, oblivious to my attempts to slow him down.

Suddenly, I went limp, which got his attention. He didn't loosen his grip, but he did stop dragging me along. I stood up and stamped my foot. "I'm not getting in that truck unless you explain to me what's going on!" Unimpressed by my threat, he swept me up off the ground and carried me towards the truck.

I kicked my feet and beat my fists on top of his helmet, which hurt my hands more than his head. "Ow!" I yelled. "Now look what you made me do, you big bully!"

"Johnson! Just settle down and get your ass inside this truck, would ya?"

I would have recognized that voice anywhere. "Lucas!"

She climbed out of the truck and slapped me on the back as the MP set me down. "Welcome back to the U.S. of A.!" Lucas grabbed me in a bear hug, nearly smothering me.

"Thanks!" I gasped as I surfaced for air. "It was nice of you to arrange my transportation, but you didn't have to go to all this trouble." I straightened my hat and tucked my shirt back, attempting to regain my dignity after having made a fool of myself. "A chauffered limo would have been sufficient," I said haughtily.

"La-dee-da!" Lucas mimicked me. "I thought you might appreciate a ride to the base and my efforts to make your homecoming memorable, but you always were an ingrate," she said.

"Oh, it was memorable, all right," I said. "I should have known you were up to something when these two grabbed me." I nodded towards the MPs, who were sitting in the back of the truck having a good laugh.

"They were both in my office when I opened those Easter eggs you sent me," Lucas said. "After one sniff, they were more than happy to help me thank you for your thoughtfulness." Lucas held the door open and motioned for me to climb into the truck.

"Well, you've certainly paid me back," I said as I plopped into the front seat. "Actually, I think you overpaid me slightly and you know I'm scrupulously honest. I won't be able to sleep at night until I think of a way to repay you."

"Sweet dreams," Lucas said. She ground the gears, shifted into first and popped the clutch. We took off with a lurch. "So, you're a quitter. Tsk, tsk," she said, clucking her tongue like a disapproving Sunday-school teacher. "I never would have believed it. What happened to my pal, the future admiral, who never backed down from a challenge?"

"I'm not a quitter!" I said, stung by her accusation. "I have a plan."

"Don't tell me!" Lucas held up her hand. "You're going to get married and settle down and have babies like a normal woman, right?"

"Nope. I'm going to finish my degree and go to Officer Candidate School. Then, someday, *I'll* be the CO and nobody can tell me I can't do this and I can't do that because I'm a female person. I'll make the rules."

Lucas punched me on the shoulder. "That sounds like my old pal. I always said you'd be an admiral someday." After a few seconds, she said, "Maybe I'll go with you."

"I thought you were getting married."

"I was." Lucas answered a little too fast.

"You mean you're not?" I was surprised. She hadn't mentioned breaking her engagement. "What happened?"

"Aw, you don't want to hear the boring details," Lucas said with a shrug. "I should have known better than to trust a seagoing sailor." She was suddenly interested in something outside the window, but I saw her expression before she turned her head. I nudged her with my elbow.

"Well, at least now you won't have any reason not to go to OCS with me and be an admiral, too. Right?" I chuckled, hoping to rub off some cheer.

"We'll see," she said. "Hey! Does this look familiar?" We were passing through the main gate of Naval Station Norfolk, past the starched Marines. Just like a song from the sixties brings back nostalgic memories of a high-school dance, driving through that gate took me right back to my first day in the Fleet. My face burned as I remembered how scared and embarrassed I'd felt when I checked into the barracks and pot-bellied Petty Officer Hawkins informed me that women had three positions in the Navy— on their backs, on their bellies, or on the way out the door.

This time it would be different, though. I had been around; halfway around the world to be exact, and I came home with a few medals on my chest. No salty sailors were going to make me cry.

"What can I do for you, sweetheart?" Yeoman First-Class Kroll squinted at my check-in sheet. Kroll was in charge of the personnel department and was the leading petty officer at Fleet Logistics Support Squadron One, VR-1. All the men on board would follow his example, so I knew I had to set things straight right from the start.

I smiled sweetly at him. "You can check me on board, sugar lips."

YN1 Kroll jerked his head as if I'd slapped him. I batted my eyelashes at him. He stood and hitched up his pants as he squared his bony shoulders. "Do you realize that you're talking to an E-6—a first-class petty officer in this man's Navy?" Kroll leaned forward, a menacing scowl on his face.

"Yes, I do," I said, leaning across his desk until our faces were close enough to feel each other's breath. "And *you're* talking to an E-5—a second-class petty officer in this *woman's* Navy."

Kroll sat back down and looked me over in silence for a

few minutes. Then he signed my check-in papers and pushed them across his desk. "So, I see we got a female with a little spunk," he said, his voice noncommittal. "Maybe it'll make life more interesting around here." He stuck out his hand. "Welcome aboard."

"Thanks." I gave Kroll's hand a firm shake. "How many other Waves work here?"

"Three," he said, "but they're all lowly E-2's. They don't mingle with the rest of the crew very often." I had the definite feeling that Kroll was trying to tell me something, but he was certainly taking the long-distance route.

"Why not?"

"Oh, I don't know," he said. Like hell he didn't. "Guess Old Smitty has 'em scared or something."

"Who's Smitty?" I asked, just as Kroll intended me to. It would have been easier if he would just tell me what he had to say, but he obviously enjoyed parceling out his information.

Kroll rubbed his fingertips together. "Oh, you'll meet Smitty soon enough. I don't want to spoil the surprise," he said. "But don't worry, you can handle him. I just hope he can handle you."

"He probably can't," I said, "but neither could my father and he had a head start." Kroll's stone face finally cracked. He chuckled to himself and directed me to the administrative office, my next check-in point. As I left his office, he pointed a finger at me.

"If I were you, I wouldn't be too cocky around the new CO," he confided. "He's a good old boy and he isn't exactly crazy about females, unless they wink at him, of course."

"Of course," I sighed. Why did they let us in the Navy if no one wants us, I wondered. Maybe they just needed somebody to pick on, after regulations were made that prohibited making life miserable for ethnic minorities.

224

As I left Kroll's office on the second deck of the huge aircraft hangar that housed VR-1, a terrific roar shook the entire building. I leaned over the balcony that extended the length of the hallway. Below me, on the hangar floor, the aviation maintenance crew was fiddling with the engines of a T-39 trainer. They were wearing headsets to muffle the sound, but my unprotected ear drums were vibrating. I had been prepared to work in a training squadron where pilots practiced on the light planes and eventually worked their way up to the big C-131 transports, but I didn't expect them to fly the airplanes inside the building. That was like learning to drive a car in the garage.

I turned around to go back into the personnel office, but as I reached for the door, Kroll opened it and handed me a pair of little yellow earplugs. He shut the door and waved at me through the window.

Earplugs in place, I headed towards the admin office on the first deck. Halfway down the stairs, I had to back up against the wall to make way for four men who were carrying a vending machine upstairs. As they passed me, I could hear a man on the other side of the machine complaining.

"Goddam broads," he griped. "First they bitch about my swearing and the old man chews me out. Then they make me take down my pinup calendar and move my magazines out of the duty office." He paused while they navigated the landing, then continued his tirade. As they headed up the stairs, I could see the third-class petty-officer insignia on his left arm. "Now they got us carrying this damned contraption up to the women's head. They'll probably make us carry them damned sanitary supplies up here, too, along with the paper towels and toilet paper. Shit! It ain't manly to be walking around in broad daylight with a box of tampoons."

225

I coughed and the sailor nearest me looked up in surprise.

"Hey, Smitty," he called, "better cool it. There's a female in the vicinity."

Smitty didn't bother to look around to see who was listening. He obviously assumed I was one of the junior women at VR-1 that he scared on a regular basis. "I don't give a shit," Smitty answered. "I'm sick of broads. They just make more work for us men. They spring a leak which ain't our fault in the first place and then expect us to supply the plugs."

So this was the character that Kroll had not so subtly warned me about. Apparently, no one had told Smitty that he now had the pleasure of working with a woman who outranked him. He would undoubtedly be ecstatic to meet me, but I decided to wait a while before introducing myself. We had plenty of time to become bosom buddies. I was sure he'd like the bosom part, anyway, and once we met it would only take him a year or two to warm up to me.

Meanwhile, I decided to concentrate on finding a way to make friends with Captain Davis. He hadn't officially taken charge of the squadron yet, so there was still a chance to make a great first impression. I planned to demonstrate my professional competence by writing a superb press release about the official change-of-command ceremony. All the captain's officer friends as well as his relatives and social acquaintances were invited to observe the event.

The color guard practiced inside the hangar every afternoon for two weeks. I have never understood why official Navy attempts to impress people always include a color guard, an inspection, and a speech when they could just as easily provide an unforgettably impressive display of naval excellence by calling General Quarters.

General Quarters is a much more memorable sight than a row of waving flags and a couple of inspirational phrases. Even old veterans are newly impressed every time they see GQ in action. Here's what happens. A bunch of normal–looking guys are hanging around the ship, shooting the breeze and telling outrageous lies about the women they have conquered, when the alarm rings, signifying an emergency, like a fire on board or an enemy attack.

The loudspeaker blares "GQ! GQ!" and instantly, the crew is transformed into Super Sailors. Every one of them has a job to do—manning a fire extinguisher, opening or closing the hatches, stowing the lines, preparing the weapons on board. That's the real Navy, men hustling around the decks, responding with calm assurance in the face of catastrophe, ready to sacrifice everything, including their lives, to protect their country.

I saw Navy men spring into action at the sound of the GQ alarm a couple of times and it gave me chills. It made me proud to be in the Navy.

Captain Davis decided to stick with the traditional flag and speech motif. Before the ceremony began, the local Navy band played the usual rousing military marches. The music was so loud that conversation was impossible, so all the civilian guests fell asleep in the hot sun while waiting for the official speeches. The enlisted military personnel stood in inspection formation, cracking jokes and arguing over whose turn it was to pretend to faint during the ceremony. We kept close track of the fainting schedule. Those who "fainted" got an exciting ride to the dispensary in the ambulance, where they quickly recovered from their sunstrokes. Of course, they wouldn't be expected to endanger their health by working anymore that day.

As we discussed the fainting detail, the color guard

marched out for the national anthem and all the military folks snapped to attention.

Captain Davis marched onto the field, the sword that hung from his belt glinting in the sun, and inspected the troops. Then he shook hands with the old CO and they both made speeches about how important our mission is and how we always do a job well done. All military speeches end with the words "a job well done." It like saying "amen" after a prayer.

During the speeches, my job was to roam around and inconspicuously take photographs of the occasion. I got some good shots of Captain Davis's parents sitting in the front row, tears in their eyes, as they proudly watched the little boy who used to fly paper airplanes around their living room being sworn in as the commanding officer of a genuine naval air squadron. They wore their best Sunday clothes and sat holding hands, their grey heads close together as they admired their son.

In addition to the standard press release, I wrote a real heartwarming story for his local newspaper. "It was a proud day in the lives of Mr. and Mrs. Harlan Davis when their son, one of thirteen children, took command of Fleet Logistics Support Squadron One." I included a picture of the happy couple and used a lot of trite clichés as well as a few of my own design. The base newspaper ran the story on the front page and so did the CO's hometown paper back in Hawkinsville, Georgia. His parents were touched and Captain Davis, convinced that I was an outstanding reporter, called me to his office.

"Darned fine journalism," he boomed from across his heavy metal desk. An American flag stood behind his chair, flanked by paintings of Abraham Lincoln and Jimmy Carter. The paintings were placed so the two Presidents' faces were in line with Captain Davis's when he sat down, a trio of country boys who'd made good.

"Thank you, sir," I said, looking modestly down at my hands folded in my lap. "I'd like to ask you something while I'm here."

"What is it?" he said. Always willing to do a favor for a little lady, he was.

"I know you've worked hard to get where you are today, sir." Captain Davis nodded solemnly. "And I admire the way you inspire the troops to do their best work, sir." He nodded again. "I'm just a country girl, myself, but I'd like to be an officer just like you someday, sir." His head continued to bob up and down in approval of my desire to emulate him. "Would you endorse my application for OCS, sir?" I asked shyly.

"Why, I'd be happy to, Johnson," he said. "The Navy needs some sharp females in management."

"I think so, sir." Rising, I snapped a salute and marched out of his office.

I watched as Lucas dabbed a bit of wax on her newly acquired pool cue and sat down on her bed to polish it for the fourth time in one evening. She had finally found the perfect hobby for an incurable insomniac—billiards. Lucas had given up playing cards at night because her supervisor kept counseling her not to spend so much time at the enlisted club. He didn't believe that she went to the club because it was open late at night; he thought she went there to drink. So she switched to billiards because, as she put it, "The Navy doesn't have a rehabilitation program for people who are addicted to shooting pool."

"Well, what did you decide?" I asked. "Are you going to OCS with me?"

"I don't know, pal," Lucas said thoughtfully. "I'd have to make some serious sacrifices to go to Officer Candidate School."

"Like what?" I said. "They don't want the rest of your

life. You only have to put in a couple of years after you get your commission."

Lucas held her cue stick up to the light and turned it over, admiring its glossy finish. "Oh, that doesn't worry me," she said. "I'm just not as well equipped as you are to be a zero." Lucas liked to call officers zeros, because their pay grades ranged from O-1 up to President of the United States, while enlisted men and women went from E-1 to E-9.

"What do you mean?" I was puzzled. "You have as much military experience and education as I do."

"I know that," Lucas said. "It's the surgery that scares me."

"Surgery?" I said. "What surgery? You just fill out the application and take a few tests."

"That's true, in your case," Lucas said. She put the cue stick in her locker and carefully shut the door, then stuffed her hands in her pockets and strolled over to the window. "But it would be much harder for me."

"Why?"

"I'd have to have brain surgery so they could lower my IQ about forty points before I could qualify to be a zero!" she sputtered, breaking into hilarious laughter at her little joke.

I made a spinach-for-dinner face at Lucas. "You're so amusing," I said. She ignored my sarcasm and patted herself on the head.

"I know," she said. "Modest, too."

I gagged. "Spare me the details, please, and just tell me. Are you going to OCS with me?"

Lucas held up her hand and inspected her fingernails. "Oh, I guess I'll go," she said. She rubbed her nails on her chest and held them up for reinspection. "You'll need someone to play golf and hang around the officers' club drinking martinis with and discussing the latest operas. Besides, it'll go to your head if you get to drive around with a little flag on your car and I don't."

"You know me so well."

"And I'm still your pal. Imagine that."

I did such a good job convincing Captain Davis and Petty Officer Kroll that I was self-confident and competent that they decided to reward me with my first assignment as a supervisor, in charge of the First Lieutenant Division. It was a dubious honor, indeed, since the First Looey, as we called it, was the repository for all the problem children— the sailors waiting for dishonorable discharges, the ones that all the other supervisors refuse to have in their departments, and the ones that didn't quite fit anywhere in the organization.

Smitty was the senior man and the leader of the pack in the all-male First Looey division. As much as I wanted to be a supervisor, I wasn't sure I could handle Smitty and CO Kroll assured me that I could. On the way to introduce me formally to the men as their new supervisor, he told me that Smitty was really a teddy bear beneath his tattooed exterior.

Kroll made the standard speech about welcoming me to the organization and whispered, "They're all yours, kid." I tried, but I couldn't picture the sullen faces that ignored my cheery greeting as friendly bears. No one spoke until Kroll left the office, then Smitty spat a wad of tobacco into the trash can and addressed my left breast.

"I ain't never worked for a split-tail and I ain't gonna start today," he said. He had expected me to blush at his language, and I obliged, but he also expected me to be scared of him and I was happy to disappoint him in that respect.

I didn't blame Smitty for resenting the fact that a woman young enough to be his daughter had been assigned to supervise him. He had been in the Navy since I was in diapers, and he knew his job, but there weren't many anchors and cables to handle on shore and he wasn't interested in changing his rating just so he could be promoted. Smitty was the quintessential sailor—a master story teller and a hard worker. The other men in his division automatically looked to him to set the standard. Instinctively, I knew that, regardless of my position, if I tried to give Smitty a direct order he'd make a fool of me.

Fortunately, I had come prepared for battle. I pulled out a piece of chewing gum and slowly unwrapped it, taking my time before answering Smitty's challenge. I stuffed the gum into my mouth and chewed it for a few seconds. "You don't work for me, sailor. We both work for the Navy. I just happen to outrank you in this job." I paused to sniff and hitch up my pants by the belt buckle. "If you can't do your job, put in for a transfer and I'll approve it. If you can do your job, then we won't have any problems. I don't plan to change anything around here. Looks like you have everything under control, don't you?" I sniffed and looked around the room, meeting each man's gaze without flinching.

Smitty chawed quietly, as his eyes traveled from my shoes to my face, pausing to take in each detail. He looked me in the eye for a full minute without blinking or speaking. I forced myself to hold his gaze, grinding my teeth into my gum, until Smitty spat a wad of tobacco into the trash can and ran his tongue over his front teeth. "Well," he said solemnly, "I guess I could give it a try just for a while."

I was standing close enough to spit my gum into the trash can. Bull's-eye! I nodded at Smitty, looked around at

232

the other men, sniffed, and swaggered out of the office and down the hall into the women's head. Inside, I scowled at myself in the mirror. Then I hitched up my pants and swaggered a few steps forward before I collapsed into a chair and laughed until my aching stomach refused to take another guffaw.

I splashed some cold water on my face, straightened my necktie, and brushed a speck of lint off my collar. I couldn't waste all afternoon in the women's head. No, sir. I had to get back to my office. After all, I had a job to do in this man's Navy.